THE
NORTHAMPTON
& HARBOROUGH
LINE

Northampton Castle - the original station, shewing the track layout, the short platforms, the West Bridge, and the high fences of the Nene viaduct at 62 chains (Northamptonshire Libraries)

THE NORTHAMPTON & HARBOROUGH LINE

John Gough

RAILWAY AND CANAL
HISTORICAL SOCIETY
1984

For
E.M.H.

First published 1984 by the Railway and Canal Historical Society
Registered Office: 12 High Street, Oakham, Leicestershire LE15 6AW

ISBN 0 901461 35 0

Typeset by Moorland Publishing Co Ltd, Ashbourne, Derbyshire.
Printed by Dotesios (Printers) Ltd, Bradford on Avon, Wilts.

Contents

Illustrations

Author's Note

The railway between Northampton and Market Harborough did not pass through dramatic scenery, involved no substantial engineering works, and was never the scene of unusual locomotive or rolling stock workings. No romantic trains ran this way. Yet this was a branch with a rich and complex history closely tied up with the politics of the formative years of two of the greatest of the pre-Grouping railway companies, the London & North Western and the Midland. What might have been no more than a rural branch-line was then involved less than two decades after its opening in more inter-company rivalry, which led to its fulfilling a role never dreamed of when first it carried traffic. This was a line worth study in its own right, and also worth study as a tiny fragment of the history of the company that many would regard as pre-eminent in the days before the creation of the Big Four, the London & North Western Railway. We still wait for someone to write the definitive history of that company.

Although this book includes a strip map to shew the route of the various proposals for lines between Northampton and Market Harborough, there is no large folding map of the area. The most useful map to set the railway in context and to identify the various places mentioned is the Ordnance Survey One-Inch Seventh Series Sheet 133, Northampton. Greater detail can be found on the relevant 1:25000 sheets (the 2½ inch sheets). These are SP75-78, Northampton (South), Northampton (North), Brixworth, and Market Harborough. As far as annotation is concerned, a policy of 'light referencing' has been followed, with an attempt being made to give enough information for anyone wishing to do so to identify all the sources used whilst trying to avoid cluttering up the pages with detailed references for every single statement.

Many people have helped me in various ways in the preparation of this work. Particular thanks are due to Harry Paar, Sandy Cunningham, and my wife for reading the manuscript at various stages and making helpful suggestions. The map of the proposed lines was provided for me by my colleagues Terry Garfield and Ruth Rowell, and I was helped in the making of the other diagrams by my wife and by colleagues in the Central Photographic Unit of the University of Leicester. The Newspaper Study Group of the Northamptonshire Industrial Archaeology Group very kindly placed at my disposal a wealth of information about references in the Northampton local newspapers, and Victor Hatley gave freely of his great knowledge of the history of Northampton itself. Any work of this kind relies on the facilities provided by libraries and record offices, and I am very glad to have the opportunity to thank the staffs of the Public Record Office at Kew, the Leicestershire County Record Office, the Northamptonshire County Record Office, and the Leicester University Library for their help. The bulk of the work was undertaken in the Public Record Office, that most agreeable of national reference institutions. No doubt some errors and omissions will be detected in my work, despite all my checking, and for these I alone am responsible. I should, of course, be glad to receive any corrections — or additional information — through the Railway & Canal Historical Society.

John Gough
London 1983

1

The Origins of the Line

When the railway between Northampton and Market Harborough was finally closed to all traffic in August 1981 there was every appearance that yet one more branch had come to the end of its days. However, this particular branch had a more than usually interesting history, both in its origins and in the way it later developed into a secondary main line before it finally lost almost all of its feeder routes and became a simple goods-only link between the once-rival Midland and London & North Western main lines.

Almost fifty years ago Joan Wake demonstrated that the stories that the London & Birmingham Railway had missed Northampton and instead passed through Blisworth because of the opposition of the town were quite wrong: there had been convincing engineering reasons for the choice of route finally made by the Stephensons.[1] The question was further investigated by Victor Hatley, and he shewed clearly that there is no evidence either locally in Northampton or in the Minute Books of the London & Birmingham Company itself to suggest opposition from the inhabitants of Northampton and that the apparent opposition of the Corporation of the town can most reasonably be seen as the cautious reaction of a landowner in 1830 to the possibility of a line passing over the municipal estate at Bugbrooke — land lying five miles outside the town itself. Alternative routes were indeed considered by the promoters of the London & Birmingham, and one of these passed through Northampton whilst another came very close to the town.[2]

There was even another possibility. When it became clear that the London & Birmingham line was not going to pass through Northampton it seems that the hopes of the people there turned to a railway that might link Derby, Nottingham, and Leicester with Northampton and London by way of a junction with the London & Birmingham. Such a line could also provide a route north to Manchester by way of the Cromford & High Peak Railway. In late 1830 a scheme was proposed in Derby for a 'Grand Midland Railway'. Although it is very unclear as to what came of this proposal, the idea remained alive, and it is evident that notions of a railway from Northampton to Leicester and Derby were early in the field. In his 1832 Parliamentary evidence for the London & Birmingham Robert Stephenson stated that he had actually examined the country between the London & Birmingham line and Derby. But nothing happened.

It was to be the Midland Counties Railway that raised once more the hopes of at least some people in Northampton that they might obtain a place on a main line of railway. The Midland Counties began with proposals in 1829 for a line to bring coal from the Derbyshire and Nottinghamshire coalfields to Leicester, to compete with the supplies being brought in so much more cheaply from the Leicestershire coalfield over the newly-opened Leicester & Swannington line. By the autumn of 1832 the name of 'Midland Counties Railway' had been formally adopted, and it had been decided not to end the line in Leicester but instead to head south and make a junction with the London & Birmingham main line, thus providing a through route for all classes of traffic. At this stage it seems that both Rugby and Northampton were being considered as possible points of junction. The proposals did not go forward, and by the time some replanning had been undertaken in 1833 it had been decided that the junction should be made in Rugby.[3] There were obvious attractions in this: the line would involve the shortest distance for construction south of Leicester, and therefore the least capital expenditure; the country to be traversed was not particularly difficult for the making of a railway to the standards then considered desirable; and a Rugby line would also allow a reasonable service to be given for traffic between Leicester and Birmingham.

It seems astonishing that there was so little protest from Northampton at this change of plans. Victor Hatley demonstrated that there was a strong likelihood that the promoters of the Midland Counties Railway deliberately chose their methods of publicity in such a way as to arouse the least notice in Northampton. He suggested that the business community of the town was not perhaps as awake as it ought to have been in examining the newspapers for news of what was going on in the new world of railways, and he drew attention to the admission of one leading Northampton banker that he scarcely ever saw the London papers.

Not until 1836 did the Midland Counties scheme finally go to Parliament — and it was not until 1836 that Northampton and Market Harborough, both of which faced economic loss as a result of the choice of the Rugby route, seem to have accepted the need to initiate some sort of action. Northampton was the point at which the two principal roads between London and Leicester divided. The earlier route ran north through Welford and entered the heart of Leicester by the roads that had led through the old gates. These, which were narrow and an impediment to traffic, had not been demolished until 1774. But already in the late sixteenth and early seventeenth centuries this road had been superseded in importance by the alternative route through Kelmarsh, Market Harborough, and Kibworth, which had the advantage of bringing its traffic to an important trading area of Leicester without the need to pass through the gates. In 1726 this road had been turnpiked through Leicestershire and substantial improvements had then been made to it, such as the by-pass for Kibworth Harcourt. Market Harborough, which probably owes its origins to its place on this road, and which — like Kibworth — obtained its market soon after 1200, had replaced Hallaton by the later Middle Ages as the principal town of southern Leicestershire, and it accordingly grew in prosperity. Coaching inns, such as the *Three Swans*, were established, and in 1785 a fast mail-coach service began to operate over this route from London.[4] It was clear that if a railway were built and were to take traffic away from the old routes, then there would be serious economic consequences for the towns along those routes. Northampton and Market Harborough would both lose traffic if a railway went via Rugby.

At the beginning of 1836 Northampton awoke from its sleep and began to take action. A scheme called the 'South Midland Counties Railway' was initiated, with support largely based in Northampton and Market Harborough. Francis Giles, a noted civil engineer who at the time held the post of Engineer to the London & Southampton Railway, was engaged to make a survey for a route from the London & Birmingham main line through the two towns to Leicester. Interestingly, there was another project in the 'Little Mania' of 1836 that was designed to connect with the line through Market Harborough. This was the Cambridge Transverse Railway, which would have run from Harborough through Kettering, Huntingdon, and St Ives to Cambridge and beyond.

Because of the agitation from the supporters of the South Midland Counties plan, the land was also examined by Charles Vignoles, the Engineer of the Midland Counties Railway, who stirred up some ill-feeling amongst local landowners by some very tactless surveying and who estimated that a line through Northampton would cost about half a million pounds more than the line to Rugby. Nevertheless, it was possible to force the Midland Counties to accept a clause in its Act forbidding construction south of the Wigston/Knighton boundary just south of Leicester for a year to allow time for a full investigation of the rival scheme for the southern connection.[5] There was still a great deal to play for.

Publicity certainly began to appear in some quarters. A paper was issued on 16 February 1836 in Market Harborough which set out to make a comparison between the two possible routes between Leicester and the South.[6] Naturally the argument advanced here was in favour of the Harborough and Northampton route of the South Midland Counties plan, and the point was made that of the two objectives of the promoters of the Midland Counties (to provide a route to London, and also to allow traffic to pass west to Birmingham) the minor objective (that of serving west-bound traffic) would be better achieved by the direct line from Derby to Birmingham that was being promoted at the same time. As far as the major objective of the traffic to and from London was concerned, it was stated that 'the natural Line [was] by Harborough, and if not immediately, must, in the progress of improvements, be ultimately adopted'. The great advantages of the line, both in terms of the greater local traffic to be obtained and in terms of the more direct through route, were strongly emphasized, and attention was forcibly drawn to the importance of the possible cattle traffic for the London market from the grazing district between Leicester and Northampton. As a rhetorical question it was asked whether the Directors of the Midland Counties Railway would preclude the benefit of taking forty-three miles of country which must be infinitely more profitable per mile than any other part of their line. That was the one side of the argument. The other was the loss to Market Harborough, since the traffic it enjoyed by road would fall off and not be replaced:

> The Commercial part of the community are now fully alive to the advantages of Railways, and it must be said, to the credit of Harborough, that although rather late in the field, its Inhabitants are now exerting themselves to the utmost, to avoid the ruinous state of things that threaten them, — and certainly with the brightest prospects of success.
>
> The diversion from the Road through Harborough of coaches and other conveyances which now contribute in various ways to the support of its population, would not only be hurtful in that sense, but would have also the effect of greatly lessening the consumption of Hay and horse Corn, and thus would be injurious to the landed interest in the neighbourhood.

The author went on to refer to the fact that estimates of traffic were being made and that an eminent engineer had been engaged to make a survey. He asserted that the line through Harborough would be better for the public and better for the shareholders, and would be the one that would ultimately have to be adopted.

In the time available in the Session of 1836 it was impossible for Giles to produce proper plans for his line, but an indication could be given of its nature. The line would run from a junction with the London & Birmingham main line at Courteenhall (very close to the later Roade junction) northwards through Northampton and Kelmarsh to Market Harborough. From there it would run by way of Kibworth to Leicester, where it would make its junction with the Midland Counties line and also provide a connection with the Leicester & Swannington line. Full details are to be found in the Prospectus issued in November 1836 and in the Deposited Plans.[7] It was claimed in support of this route that it would be shorter to London by five miles and could be built without a single tunnel (as well as enabling passengers to avoid the three tunnels at Weedon and the long one at Kilsby). Stamford could be reached by means of a branch (which could later be extended further to the East). And — very importantly in the light of then-prevailing attitudes — the line proposed would not interfere with any gentleman's residence. Additionally, there would be extensive local traffic from Market Harborough, Northampton, and Stamford, and it would be possible to handle the great quantities of fat cattle sent weekly from the grazing districts of Lincoln, Leicester, Rugby, and Northampton to the Smithfield Market. An interesting sideline on this point comes from the earlier paper produced in Market Harborough, in which it was pointed out that the need to drive cattle to London meant that their condition deteriorated, with the result that Londoners were receiving too great a supply of poor-quality joints and not nearly enough of the high-quality joints of meat that the market required. The coming of the railway must most certainly have greatly improved the quality of fresh foods of all sorts available in the fast-growing cities of the nineteenth century. In the Prospectus of late 1836 the estimated total cost of the line was £1.2M — a little higher than earlier suggestion had indicated.

Also in the later part of 1836 a pamphlet was published in Market Harborough by 'A Landed Proprietor' (William de Capell Brooke, it is suggested by Mr Hatley) expressing the hope that the landed proprietors of the area might review their opposition to the proposed South Midland Counties Line and strongly arguing once again the point of view that 'the project of the Midland Counties Company [has] for its object the total diversion of the old and accustomed traffic through Harborough and Northampton'.[8] A little later the author writes:

> The other certain results must be, that the whole traffic which has for so long a period passed through from the Metropolis to the Northern districts, via to Northampton, Harborough, and Leicester, besides considerable traffic in other directions, the whole forming an aggregate of enormous amount, will in the short period of 4 or 5 years from this time, be intercepted, diverted entirely from the county, and transferred to another district, to the ruin, aye, utter ruin of hundreds who have vested their little capital in the present line of road.

The author continues to point out the significance of the railway for the agricultural community, and also the possibility that the railway would bring of much-reduced coal prices in the towns, another matter that can be seen to have been of great importance from the frequency of reference to it not only in railway company records but also in the evidence in Parliamentary proceedings. His principal concern is with Market Harborough, and his conclusion as to the effect of missing the railway is a dramatic one:

> What will be the condition of Market Harborough when she has lost the whole of her trade? why that she will soon become a deserted, lonesome, dirty, country village, as dull as Kelmarsh or Lamport, and honest folkes that come after us will aske the reason why she had once the word 'Market' tacked to her name. Her tradesmen ruined, her manufacture lost, one little gingerbread fair in the year, the population unable to find employment, the rent of land greatly reduced, in a short time she will be abandoned by all, with any capital remaining, in order to save themselves from total ruin.

Such was the threat to those on the traditional route of communication, it appeared. As we have seen, time was obtained, and Giles was able to go ahead and prepare full plans for the Session of 1837. A Bill was duly deposited, and it received its First Reading in due course. But it was passed to a Committee investigating Railway Subscription Lists,[9] and the scheme collapsed when it was discovered that many of its subscribers were but men of straw. Standing Orders required half the capital (£1.2M for this scheme) to be subscribed, and the actual amount taken up in this case appeared to be £606,200 — but of this, £158,150 turned out on examination not to be bona fide. Thus Standing Orders were not complied with and the scheme collapsed. Even as early as 18 February 1837 all the members except one of the Leicester Committee for the South Midland Counties, of which John Ellis (later Chairman of the Midland Railway) was a member, resigned all

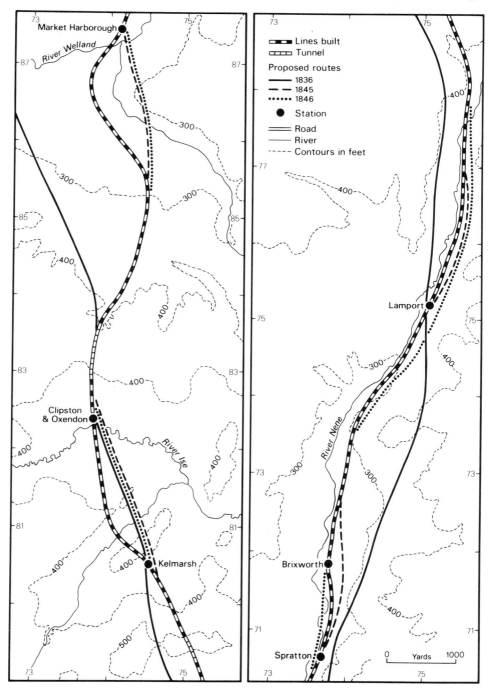

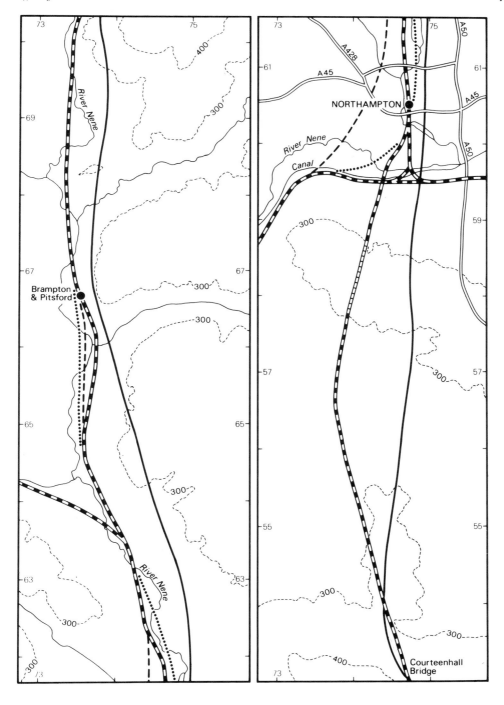

connection.[10] So it was the line to Rugby that was built. Northampton was not to have its main line yet. One significant fact that emerges from the evidence that the Committee on Subscription Lists took is that the rise in the cost of the main scheme as against the estimates of 1836 (from £0.9M to £1.1M for the main line without its branches) was to be accounted for by the greater cost of moving earth, the greater cost of land, and the greater cost of rails. Time was teaching the railway engineers some lessons.

Giles's plan is an interesting one, and surprisingly little known, even though the Deposited Plans are available for consultation and there is a detailed description by Francis Whishaw in his 1837 book *Analysis of Railways*.[11] Any railway between Northampton and Leicester must effectively follow the route through Market Harborough: a direct line through Welford is not an attractive possibility on account of the severe gradients that would be involved. From Northampton the valley of the Nene can be followed to a mile or so north of the Maidwell to Draughton road, giving easy gradients. But then the river changes direction and the railway continuing northwards has to cross a ridge of high ground separating the Nene valley, which runs from north to south, from the Ise valley, which takes a west to east course. Another ridge of high ground near Great Oxendon separates the Ise valley from the much broader Welland valley, also generally running eastwards. Continuing northwards, there is another ridge at Kibworth, which can be reached and left by following river valleys. There is an useful investigation, though unfortunately based on incomplete information, of railway topography in this area by Philip Martin, who discusses the reasons why the small town of Rothwell never obtained a railway station.[12]

Any railway engineer must decide on the general level of his line so as to achieve reasonable gradients while ensuring that the quantities of material to be excavated from the cuttings balance as far as possible the quantities to be tipped for the embankments — and can be taken over the shortest possible distance to form those embankments. The total quantity of earth to be moved depends both on the nature of the country and on the capital investment the railway is prepared to make in order to buy an easily-graded line with its subsequent lower working costs. There is always the alternative of accepting lower standards of construction in order to save on capital outlay and to get the line into service sooner, but the consequence of this, especially if it is envisaged that the line will carry heavy traffic, will be much higher running costs. Very often it was necessary in later years to improve routes that had been built to standards lower than desirable in order to solve considerable operational problems, and the eventual Midland main line between Leicester and Bedford is a good example of this. Such improvements could involve not only considerable capital outlay but also a good deal of operational difficulty whilst they were in progress. In the early days of the railways there was a further complication: little faith was placed in the power of the early locomotives to ascend gradients (or in the power of brakes to check trains running down steep banks!). It was also held desirable to have curves of as wide a radius as possible. It is certainly no accident that our earliest main lines have gentle gradients and easy curves and are so often those best suited to high-speed operation today.

The route chosen by Francis Giles was a typical early railway. After a descent from the junction with the London & Birmingham line to Northampton at 1:264, the ruling gradient was to be no more than 1:377, as can be seen from the sections (pp 24-5). To achieve this it was necessary, after branching out of the London & Birmingham line at Courteenhall, to keep at a high level through Northampton, crossing more than sixty feet above the water level of the Grand Union Canal, and then, as indicated on the map (pp12-13), to keep to relatively high ground by running on the upper slopes of the eastern side of the Nene valley as far as Lamport before crossing to the west side to pierce the first ridge by a short tunnel at Kelmarsh. (Thus the Deposited Plans prove that there would have been a tunnel to travel through after all!) From Kelmarsh the railway would have run in a virtually straight line, keeping to high ground where possible, through Great Oxendon, just west of Market Harborough, to Foxton and then to Kibworth, where it would have been more-or-less on the same location as the Midland line that was finally built. The requirement for good gradients dictated the need to keep at high level in the vicinity of Market Harborough, and so the major obstacle was the crossing óf the Welland. This would have been no less than seventy-two feet under the railway at the point of crossing. Market Harborough would have boasted a viaduct as dramatic as that of Stockport, though not quite so centrally located. The same need for height meant that Giles planned the only line that would have run on the west side of Market Harborough, as all other engineers, operating at a lower level, chose to follow the valley of the Welland where it runs briefly from south to north through Little Bowden and Great Bowden. Giles's line would certainly have been eminently suitable for fast running in later times. But the works would have been immense. As it was, the Rugby section of the Midland Counties line, on which work could duly begin in 1837, involved significantly heavier works than the northern section in order to keep good gradients, and therefore higher construction costs per mile.[13] The works of the South Midlands Counties Railway would have been vastly heavier and much more expensive still.

It was perhaps inevitable that some version of the South Midland Counties scheme should have been resurrected during the Railway Mania of 1845-6. On 28 April 1845 a committee on which Northampton interests were strongly represented met, and it decided that measures should be taken for the building of a line from the London & Birmingham near Northampton to the Midland Railway near Syston, together with a branch to Leicester.[14] (The Midland had been formed in 1844 by an amalgamation of the Midland Counties line with the North Midland, which ran on from Derby to Leeds, and with the Birmingham & Derby Junction Railway, which had been in fierce competition with the Midland Counties for London traffic from the North Midland.) The committee, whose members included John and Samuel Percival (John being the Northampton banker who had admitted in the Parliamentary hearings for the Midland Counties Bill back in 1836 that he did not regularly see the London newspapers), appointed a Solicitor, and steps were taken to seek the advice of Francis Giles, since he had been the Engineer for the earlier South Midland Counties proposal. The co-operation of both the larger companies in the area, the London & Birmingham and the Midland, was obtained.

By June the company, which was known at this stage as 'The South Midland or Northampton and Leicester Railway', was advertising in the *Railway Times*, where its capital was stated to be £1,000,000 in shares of £20.[15] Promises of money appear to have been readily forthcoming, as it was announced that no further applications would be entertained after 19 June, such had been the demand for the shares. The advantages of the line appeared to be many and obvious. It was to form in conjunction with railways both existing and projected the shortest practicable route between London and the East Midlands, Lancashire, the West Riding, and most of the manufacturing towns of northern England. Quite apart from the saving in distance there would be a great saving of time, since the delays at Rugby (which were already great and inconvenient, and which were likely to grow worse with the opening of the Trent Valley and the Oxford & Rugby lines — especially as the latter would make Rugby a meeting-point of the broad and narrow gauges) could be avoided. Southern and south-western traffic would still have to pass over the Leicester to Rugby line, but it would be sensible to separate off the London traffic and take it by another route. A short branch railway would remedy the lack of a connection between the Midland line and the Leicester & Swannington, and in general the supply of coal from both the Leicestershire and the Derbyshire fields to central England and to London would be greatly improved.

Tunnels were still a matter of interest: the new line would 'also avoid the Kilsby and Weedon tunnels, on the Birmingham Railway (the former of which is upwards of one mile and a quarter in length), thus combining greater security with increased expedition'. There is no mention of the fact that the substantial tunnels at Linslade, Northchurch, Watford, and Primrose Hill, each presumably with its attendant dangers, would still have to be traversed, as would the three tunnels — albeit short ones — proposed for the new line itself! From the estimates of potential traffic that had been made it was asserted that the line was likely to pay 12%. And once again normal railway matters received their comment, in that it was stated that there would be no great engineering difficulties and that there would be no interference with ornamental property. The landowners' attitude, indeed, was considered to be favourable.

An approach for engineering advice was made to Robert Stephenson in July. By the end of the month the committee, which was now strongly under Midland influence (and therefore under the influence of George Hudson, the Midland's enigmatic Chairman), communicated with the Northern & Eastern Railway about the possibility of meeting the Hitchin & Bedford and the Cambridge & Huntingdon lines, thus proposing to enter the territory of a rival scheme, the Leicester & Bedford — yet another Mania scheme, and this one strongly supported by parties favourable to the proposals for a direct railway between London and York,[16] which Hudson was doing his best to fight off. Agreement was reached in August between the Midland and the South Midland that the estimated capital, which had now risen to £1.7M, should be divided £900,000 to the South Midland and £800,000 to the Midland, with each party to make available 2,500 shares for the landowners between Market Harborough and Bedford. A month later George Hudson became company Chairman.

Matters then proceeded normally, but the Bill for the main South Midland scheme (the Northampton line, together with the branch to Bedford that had by then been acquired in the course of opposition to the Leicester & Bedford) was rejected by Commons Committee when Robert Stephenson let it be known that the intention was to send traffic on from Bedford over the line to Bletchley rather than build a continuation of the new line towards Hitchin. The rival Leicester & Bedford (which was to form a link with the proposed direct line between London and York) was rejected in the Lords, after strenuous Midland opposition. Indeed, its supporters claimed that the very strength of the Midland opposition was a measure of the essential soundness of the scheme. With the failure of both lines it was time to look to plans for the next Session. On 29 July 1846 Hudson reported that the Midland proposed to take up the South Midland as an extension of its own line, offering South Midland shareholders Midland stock to the exact amount of their deposit of 2 guineas per share. The Midland would take over all debts, liabilities, and expenses. Meanwhile the Leicester & Bedford group were licking their wounds and wondering what they should do next. First thoughts involved the dissolution and reconstitution of the company as the Leicester and Bedford (1846) Railway,[17] with 150,000 shares of £10 each, of which the Great Northern Railway — now duly in existence — would take 75,000 at a deposit of 20/- or 10%. The scripholders were to get one £10 share in lieu of each £20 share in the old company, on payment of a further deposit of 6/- and subscribing the deeds for £10 for each share. They would be credited with 20/- as a 10% deposit on each of the new shares, 8/- being a credit arising out of the arrangement with the Great Northern and 6/- more the amount remaining of the balances of the previous Session. Such were the plans and the detailed financial arrangements which were announced in the *Railway Times* on 26 September 1846. And this time, of course, the line would go on to Hitchin to meet the Great Northern there. But by October a very different course of action had been decided upon. An arrangement had been made with the Midland. The Midland

Railway was to apply for the line and would place £40,000 stock at the disposal of the Leicester & Bedford, which would give 17/- a share at the then price if the whole of the 63,000 shares issued by the old company were admitted. The Midland would pay all expenses and was to make the line within two years. The Great Northern, for its part, would offer no Parliamentary opposition.

A full account of all these machinations is given by E. G. Barnes.[18] The Midland duly obtained powers in 1847 to build a line from Wigston, on the outskirts of Leicester and close enough to the point of junction considered by Francis Giles ten years earlier, through Market Harborough, Kettering, and Bedford to a junction with the Great Northern Railway at Hitchin, together with a line from Little Bowden to a junction in Northampton with the branch from Blisworth to Peterborough of the London & North Western Railway (successor by an 1846 amalgamation to the London & Birmingham), and a line from Pytchley, just south of Kettering, to Huntingdon. In 1845/6 the question of whether to make the junction in Northampton or to run independently to the London & Birmingham main line had at first been open, but by the time that the Parliamentary Plans were drawn up in November 1845 the question had been settled in favour of Northampton, and this was also the situation in the plans of November 1846. However, none of these lines was built, despite the promises to get on with the work within two years. Money was tight, and plans for a link at Hitchin with the proposed Hertford to Hitchin line of the Eastern Counties Company — of which Hudson was also Chairman — were foiled by Parliament when it inserted clauses into the Act requiring the Midland trains to connect with those of the Great Northern at Hitchin and effectively forbidding them to run across to link up with the proposed Eastern Counties line and give an alternative route to London.[19] Then Hudson himself fell from grace, and so once again Northampton failed to obtain its place on a main line.

The surveys for the South Midland scheme in its final manifestation and for the Midland Railway Bill for the 1847 Session had been made by Robert Stephenson and Charles Liddell.[20] The former is well enough known, but the latter is also an interesting figure in the world of railway engineering. He worked on the Rugby & Stamford line of the London & North Western, and he was later involved in the Midland's Leicester & Hitchin line of 1853 and its Bedford to London line a decade later. He also planned the last of the great London lines, the Manchester, Sheffield & Lincolnshire's London Extension of the eighteen-nineties. As the map and sections shew, the plans of Stephenson and Liddell were very different from those of Giles, especially relative to the crossing of the high ground of the watershed south of Market Harborough. Only near Arthingworth would the earlier and later routes have had a section more-or-less in common. By the mid-1840s engineering views had changed, and much steeper gradients were tolerated.

Stephenson and Liddell surveyed a line that would, like Giles's, have had no sharp curves, and so would have been well enough suited to fast running on its downhill and level sections. But the ruling gradient of the climb south from Market Harborough was to be $1:117\frac{1}{2}$ in the 1845 plans, and as steep as 1:100 in the 1846 plans. The northbound climb would not have been so steep, at 1:173 (1845) and 1:165 (1846). By use of the steeper gradients it was possible to keep the line closer to the natural ground level and so to cut construction costs by reducing the scale of the earthworks. In the Nene valley the line kept closer to river level, and this meant that it did not have to begin with such a high level in Northampton itself, thus making for much easier arrangements in the town. Also, of course, a lower starting-level was dictated by the need to make a junction with the valley-bottom Blisworth & Peterborough line which had finally given Northampton its first railway connection, though only by means of a branch line, in 1845. There was only one point where the 1845 and the 1846 plans differed significantly in their courses, and that was in the route selected through Northampton itself over a distance of perhaps a couple of miles. They did, however, differ slightly in their gradients, indicating alterations broadly designed to cut the costs of the 1846/7 line by keeping closer to ground level where possible while still attempting to provide a good main line by the standards that had then become acceptable. By the time the next scheme was produced the need for a main line was gone, and what was proposed was very different. Had the 1836/7 line been built, or the 1845/7 line, then it is possible that the modern railway history of Northampton might have been very different. The building of the 1853 line in a sense made the developments of the 1960s and 1970s inevitable, to the permanent disadvantage of Northampton.

REFERENCES

1   Joan WAKE, *Northampton Vindicated or Why the Main Line Missed the Town*, published by the author, Northampton, 1935
2   Victor A. HATLEY, 'Northampton Re-vindicated: More Light on Why the Main Line Missed the Town', *Northamptonshire Past and Present* II(6), 1959, pp. 305-9
3   For a full and authoritative discussion with detailed references see Victor A. HATLEY, 'Northampton Hoodwinked? How a Main Line of Railway Missed the Town a Second Time', *Journal of Transport History* VII(3), 1966, pp. 160-72
4   J. SIMMONS, 'Communication and Transport', in N. PYE (Ed.), *Leicester and its Region*, Leicester University Press, 1972, pp. 311-24, especially pp. 313-15
5   6 William IV, cap. lxxviii, clause 7
6   RAIL 1015/2 (No. 84)
7   Prospectus RAIL 1075/432, Deposited Plans LRO QS 73/16
8   'A LANDED PROPRIETOR', *Address to the Land Owners, Land Occupiers, and Others who have signed a Petition to the House of Commons against The Proposed Line of Railroad from Leicester through Harborough and Northampton to Blisworth*, Thomas Abbot, Market Harborough, 1836. p. 4
9   RAIL 1124/11 *Fourth Report from the Select Committee on Railway Subscription Lists*, 1837
10 *ibid.* Question 12,971
11 Francis WHISHAW, *Analysis of Railways*, John Weale, 1837, pp. 220-25
12 Philip R. MARTIN, 'Rothwell; The Railway Station that never was', *Northamptonshire Past and Present* VI (3), 1980, pp. 161-4
13 Francis WHISHAW, *The Railways of Great Britain and Ireland*, 2nd edition, John Weale, 1842, p. 327
14 RAIL 637/1
15 *Railway Times*, 14 June 1845, p. 850
16 *ibid.* 5 July 1845, p. 957
17 *Railway Chronicle*, 26 September 1846, p. 947
18 E. G. BARNES, *The Rise of the Midland Railway 1844-1874*, George Allen & Unwin, 1966, pp. 80-85
19 10&11 Victoria, cap. cxxxv, clauses 55 and 58
20 Deposited Plans LRO QS 73/102 and 108

2

An Act Obtained

During 1851 a large mineral field of ironstone was discovered in Northamptonshire, and George Carr Glyn reported from the Chair to the London & North Western half-yearly meeting on 20 February 1852 that this ironstone would meet the needs of the industry in South Staffordshire and would lead to a considerable increase in the local traffic from the one district to the other.[1] The discovery was brought to the attention of the Midland Board in a different way: a meeting on 7 April 1852 received a letter from Mr J. L. Douglass, a Market Harborough solicitor who had been one of the proponents of the Leicester & Bedford scheme in 1845 and 1846, asking the Company to build the Leicester & Hitchin line.[2] Douglass pointed out that the line ought certainly to be remunerative on account of the recently-discovered ironstone deposits, which were of great extent. This was a new factor since the dropping of the earlier plans, and Douglass indicated that if the Midland did not this time build the line, then there might very well be others who would proceed instead. On the same day the Board received what its Chairman, John Ellis of Leicester, who had succeeded to that position on the downfall of Hudson, later described to a Shareholders' Meeting as one of the most influential deputations he ever attended.[3] This deputation urged that the line should be built 'either with or without a Branch from Market Harborough to Northampton as may be hereafter determined', and it stressed that if the Midland did not build the line, then there was every intention of forming a separate company to do so. The Midland's territorial interests left it with little choice, and on 5 May the Board formally resolved to seek powers for a line from Leicester through Bedford to Hitchin or another convenient place on the Great Northern main line, resolving further that if the Act were obtained the line should be built within the time allowed. The application to Parliament was to be promoted by and under the control of the Midland.

The Board explained to the shareholders in the Directors' Report that the building of the line was necessary, and that it could be accomplished more cheaply than had been envisaged in 1846/7. Moreover, the existence of the ironstone would greatly increase the original estimates of traffic.[4] Part of the way in which costs were to be cut was the elimination of the two long branches, to Northampton and to Huntingdon. What had happened is interesting. The earliest plan had been for a Northampton to Leicester line in 1836, and there had also at that time been the plan of the Cambridge Transverse Railway to join such a line at Market Harborough. In 1845 the main line of the South Midland scheme had again been a Northampton to Leicester line, to which had been added, through various political pressures connected with the need to resist the Leicester & Bedford and its Great Northern supporters, the line to Bedford and a branch to Huntingdon. But in the 1846 plans which actually became the Act of 1847 it was the line between Hitchin and Leicester that was clearly regarded as the main line, and the branches were the lines to Northampton and to Huntingdon (together, of course, with the short curves to the London & North Western in

Wellingborough). Thus the status of Northampton in the scheme had diminished considerably even in 1847, and it is not really surprising to see James Ley Douglass in 1852 clearly intent on getting the Hitchin line and referring to that to Northampton merely as a branch which might or might not be made. The Midland's determination to act at once in 1852 was shewn by the immediate formation of a committee of five directors to superintend the carrying out of the work. Formal instructions were given to the Company's Solicitor on 2 November 1852 to prepare the Bill,[5] and the Act was obtained in the ensuing Session of Parliament. Construction began at once, and the Leicester & Hitchin Railway was opened in 1857.

At this period the Midland was, of course, in a very close relationship with the London & North Western, over which company's line its entire London traffic was carried from Rugby. So close indeed was the relationship that in 1852 the two companies were actually considering amalgamation, and in these circumstances it was only natural that the Midland should let the LNW know at once of its plans with regard to the Hitchin line. This was done by letter on 5 May 1852. The Midland Secretary wrote that his company was promoting the line to protect the interests of both companies, and he added that 'a strong opinion was therefore expressed by the Board, that a participation in the Capital required for the undertaking, should be offered to the London & North Western Railway Company.'[6] Not surprisingly, the news was not exactly welcome to the LNW, which not only gave formal expression to its regrets but also stated its hopes that a review of the position of the two companies would persuade the Midland to reconsider its decision. It felt that the proposed line would not only not be consistent with the 1849 Agreement between the two companies — which contained clauses precluding either side from adopting or even encouraging measures which might divert traffic from the other company or 'prejudicially affect the interests of the other' — but would also be positively harmful to their interests. The *Railway Times* for 29 May reported the upset of the Stock Exchange at rumours of a serious disagreement between the Midland and the LNW, but commented that the matter was not likely to be a great one. A week later it commented: 'The "rupture" which last week threw some of our more nervous friends on 'Change into hysterics, is found to have had its origin in some negociations respecting the construction of the Leicester and Bedford.' It seems that 'leaks' were as common in the 1850s as they are in the 1980s! The fact that such leaks might not always be entirely accurate is shewn by the next sentence of the report, which read: 'This line, which would give the Midland another connection with the London and North-Western, has long been in abeyance, but there is now every likelihood of its being made; and so we hope the Midland is satisfied.' It was not the thought of another connection with its own system that disturbed the LNW.

The main concern of the LNW was very obviously that by building the Hitchin line the Midland would not only open up a new area of country to railway communication and come into competition with the LNW at such places as Wellingborough and Bedford, but would also acquire a potential alternative route to London independent of the LNW, and this was the reason for the appeal to the terms of the 1849 Agreement. But the Midland response was firm, and whilst (as it did in every letter in this correspondence) assuring the LNW of its entirely friendly intentions, it pointed out that when the Agreement referred to had been made the Midland's 1847 Act for a line to Hitchin — just such a line as was now proposed — had still been in force. And if there were to be any question of prejudicing the interests of the other party, then the LNW proposals for Hereford & Worcester and Newport & Hereford lines might be held to be prejudicial to the Midland.[7] The next step taken was on the LNW side, when that company's Committee of Special Affairs discussed the question on 10 June, having received a report from the Chairman (Carr Glyn) and the Secretary (Charles Stewart) on communications with John Ellis (for the Midland), William Henry

Whitbread (one of the principal landowners in favour of the Leicester & Hitchin line), and Robert Stephenson. The result of the Committee's deliberations was a recommendation to the Board for an immediate survey of lines from Northampton to Leicester through Market Harborough and from Northampton through Bedford to Hitchin or some other point on the Great Northern line. Steps were to be taken to ascertain the attitude of landowners along the route, especially that of the Duke of Bedford.[8] In these proposals we may once again recognize the South Midland scheme, with the continuation from Northampton giving an alternative line to that proposed by the Midland. It is of great interest in all these dealings to remember that at this time John Ellis was not only the Chairman of the Midland but was also a Director of the London & North Western. His main loyalties lay clearly with the former, but he did have a foot in both camps and an interest in seeing good relations between the two companies sustained.

The LNW Board met two days later, on 12 June, and wrote to the Midland, the letter being discussed by that Board on 14 July. The LNW admitted the Midland's point that there had been some discussion of the Hitchin line at a meeting between representatives of the two companies in the Midland & LNW Joint Committee during April, but noted that the only LNW Director present had been Thomas Smith, the Deputy Chairman. The Company had received no *official* notification before the letter of 5 May. The Board agreed that opposition to a possible newcomer into the territory of the two companies was sensible, but suggested that this could best be done by the lines the LNW was now proposing to connect the important parts of the district with one another and with the two systems. These lines were better than the one proposed by the Midland, which would pass through the least populous areas. And the Midland was duly offered the opportunity to participate in the LNW plans.

There was a prompt Midland reply, pointing out that the district had been surveyed by Robert Stephenson, the Engineer-in-Chief to both companies, in 1845 and 1846. Out of this had come the Rugby & Stamford Act for the LNW and the Hitchin Act for the Midland. The Rugby & Stamford line had been built, and its construction had been much to the detriment of traffic on the Midland's Syston & Peterborough line. But the Hitchin line had not been built on account of shortage of money. The Midland Directors claimed that it was still their right to occupy the district already allotted to them, and they believed that the line from Leicester to Hitchin as proposed was the best way of doing this. Moreover, they were pledged to the landowners and would have to proceed. No more is known about the LNW proposals, and it may be assumed that whatever investigations were undertaken amongst the landowners cannot have been very rewarding, for by 8 October the matter had resolved itself into a proposal for a new LNW line from Northampton to Market Harborough only.[9] The route that had been suggested is not without interest, however. One of the suggestions for the original London & Birmingham line had involved a railway from London through Baldock, Bedford, and Northampton itself, and we have seen how Robert Stephenson admitted in 1832 that he had considered a line north from Northampton to Derby. Schemes did have an astonishing tendency to resurrect themselves.

It was now the Midland's turn to be upset. There had been a meeting between the two companies on 3 September in connection with the amalgamation proposals, and the first draft of an Agreement which the LNW had submitted to the Midland representatives had contained a reference to the Leicester & Hitchin line. At the Midland's request, all mention of this was deleted, on the grounds that the Midland was already pledged to the landowners, and indeed the revised clause of the Agreement as approved went so far as to express the hope that an Agreement might be made with the Great Northern Company.[10] Thus it seems that the LNW accepted the Midland commitment. Now at this meeting there was no mention of the LNW proposal for the

Northampton & Harborough line, and on 9 November John Ellis, wearing his hat as Midland Chairman, wrote to Thomas Smith to state the views and feelings of the Midland about this proposal. As a result, the whole question was considered in detail by the full LNW Board on 13 November. The view which emerged was that the Midland had been under a misapprehension about the LNW position, and the group of directors that had met the Midland representatives on 3 September was instructed to re-convene and meet the Midland again to explain that the LNW was in fact acting in strict conformity with the Agreement that had been made. This meeting duly took place in the Queen's Hotel in Birmingham on 26 November, and in due course its results were considered by both Boards. On 1 December the Midland, still dissatisfied, formally resolved that the LNW scheme was an infraction of the Agreement, stating that it might be used in Parliament as an argument against the Leicester & Hitchin and that as the line was in any case worthless in itself in terms of any possible return on capital it ought not to be proceeded with. The LNW was duly urged to abandon its plans.

On 11 December it was the turn of the LNW Board to meet, and, needless to say, the view it took was rather different. Sincere regrets were expressed that a misunderstanding had arisen from the fact that there had been no specific mention of the Northampton & Market Harborough line at the meeting on 3 September, but it was felt that the matter had been overlooked by both sides and that neither side should either accept or impute blame. In detail, it was argued that as the line had been entered upon prior to 3 September and as its prosecution was not inconsistent with an absence of opposition to the Leicester & Hitchin scheme, the Board could not admit that this promotion went against either the letter of the Agreement or its spirit. As to the Midland's specific objections, it was felt that the apprehension that the scheme might be used as an argument against the Midland proposal was unconvincing, as in the past both lines had already received Parliamentary sanction (in the 1847 Act). Although there was room for some difference of opinion as to the probable return on outlay, the question of a partial loss of interest on £180,000 of capital could not be a matter for serious consideration when regarded in connection with questions involving the interests of upwards of fifty millions and with the arrangements and character of a large company. The Board could not see the projection of the line as dangerous to the Amalgamation Bill: rather its abandonment would be highly impolitic, as it would give the opponents of the amalgamation the only weapon that was likely to prevail in Parliament, which was that such measures could tend to withhold from towns and districts the means of communication that they might obtain if the amalgamation of large companies were not to be permitted. Having thus rehearsed its arguments, the Board re-affirmed its total commitment to the aims agreed on 3 September, stating that amalgamation offered the best hopes for the future prosperity of both companies.[11]

Although the Midland was not entirely happy with this when it discussed the matter again on 5 January 1853, it appears to have pursued the matter no further, and certainly the amalgamation proposals do not appear to have hesitated either. Perhaps, however, the air of injured innocence taken by the LNW does ring a trifle hollow: it is quite clear from that company's records that it was spurred into action by the news that the Midland was to take up the Leicester & Hitchin again, even though it did have its eyes on the potential ironstone traffic in the area very early in 1852. And there is an interesting comment in the *Railway Times* about the LNW plans for the 1853 Session, that: 'Not one of the schemes . . . is urgently required. There was no stir for any of them (the Worcester and Hereford excepted) until the London and North-Western emissaries appeared in the various localities, and the other essentials to agitations were adopted.'[12]

Whatever the arguments, it is clear that by the spring of 1853 the LNW had a clear field for its plans in the Northampton area. It is also clear that the nature of the railway to be built was quite different from what had earlier been envisaged. The plans of the 1830s and the 1840s for a line over this ground had envisaged that line as a part of a main route from London to the East Midlands and beyond, and its engineering would have been in keeping with such aspirations. But we have seen that in the hands of the LNW the plans were soon limited to a simple connection between Northampton and Market Harborough only — and thus to a link between the two LNW branch-lines already in existence, the Northampton & Peterborough and the Rugby & Stamford. Such a link may be considered logical enough, but it was scarcely likely to be the main line once envisaged. And the engineering plans reflect this, even though once again Robert Stephenson was responsible for them.[13] (His erstwhile partner over this ground, Charles Liddell, was busy with the Midland's Leicester & Hitchin line — the other half of the old South Midland project.) The changes to the gradients of the 1845-7 plans were slight, with the ruling gradient southbound being eased to 1:105 (though the length of the climb was increased), and the ruling gradient northbound being significantly increased to 1:100. In the valley south of Lamport various minor changes of level took place, to give a 'rougher' gradient profile, and the curvature of the line was considerably increased. Naturally at the north end of the line the junction was moved to link with the LNW line from Rugby rather than the Midland's proposed line to Kettering and the south. The result of these changes was to keep the line closer to ground level, and thus to cut down even further on the amount of earthworks required (see sections), so making construction cheaper and easier — though in one way at least these decisions were a potential addition to costs, as will be seen. A glance at the Ordnance Survey 1:25000 sheets of the district shews clearly that as built a great deal of the line was actually located at ground level, a number of slight changes to the plans having been made during construction, as was normal.

The plan taken to Parliament was for a line 18 miles long, together with an east-facing connecting line in Northampton itself, and the estimated cost was £250,000. This was a relatively low amount, and a comparison with the low figure of £15,000 a mile allowed for the Leicester & Hitchin is interesting.[14] The LNW Special Meeting of Proprietors to consider the plans before Parliament for the Session was held on 30 April 1853, and the circular sent round in advance by the Directors stated that:

> The Northampton and Market Harborough branch is identical with the project sanctioned by Parliament in the year 1847. The line is supported by the town of Northampton, and the landed proprietors of the district — now become still more important by the recent discovery of iron ore, of excellent quality, and in great abundance.[15]

At the meeting itself, General Anson, who had succeeded George Carr Glyn as the Chairman of the LNW, explained that this iron ore made it seem very probable that the line would be remunerative. He went on to say that:

> This line has been before the House of Commons already, and the most powerful proprietors in the county as well as the town of Northampton were unanimous in giving it their support. I therefore do not see how we could refuse to go on with a line once sanctioned by Parliament, again proposed, and which has been so generally called for.[16]

As far as the Parliamentary campaign of 1853 was concerned, the scheme was indeed not a contentious one. It went before the Group 'O' Committee, chaired by Mr Bankes (the Member for Dorsetshire), together with the Midland's Leicester & Hitchin line, the Great Northern's No. 1 and Bedford Bills, the Hammersmith Bill of the North & South Western Junction, and the Bill for the Oldham Branch of the LNW. In supporting the Northampton & Harborough Bill two engineers were examined, George Robert Stephenson (Robert Stephenson's nephew) and George

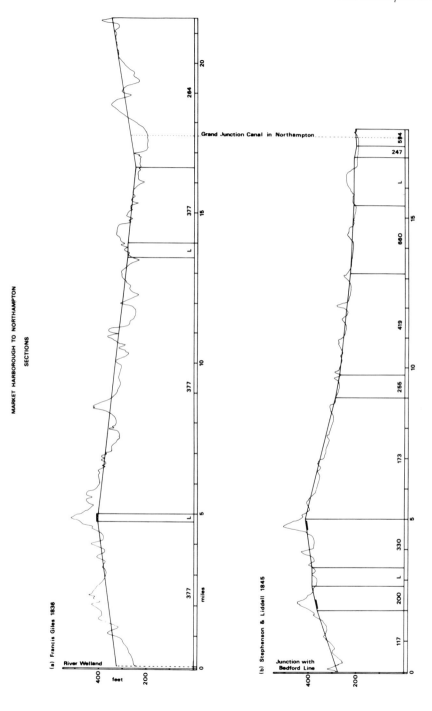

MARKET HARBOROUGH TO NORTHAMPTON
SECTIONS

(a) Francis Giles 1836

(b) Stephenson & Liddell 1845

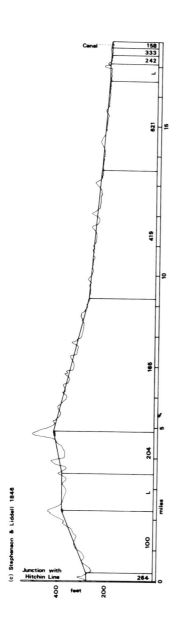

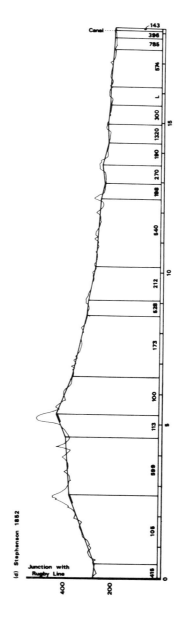

Parker Bidder, a well-known and respected civil engineer who had been retained by the LNW for parliamentary and legal work. No engineering evidence was taken in opposition. There were to be two tunnels on the line, of 462 and 484 yards respectively, and each was to be of 24-foot width. The steepest gradient would be 1:100 and the sharpest curve was of 13 chains radius. The total length of the line would be 18 miles 1 furlong 99 yards. Such were the details normally reported to the House by a Committee. The Committee also fixed charges for carrying small parcels and provided for a reduction in the charges for conveying ironstone in certain cases.[17]

The line received more opposition from certain of the LNW shareholders than it received in Parliament. It was also opposed in such periodicals as the *Railway Times*, which liked it as little as it liked the Leicester & Hitchin and also saw the two schemes as being in duplication of each other. On 25 June the LNW held its Wharncliffe Meeting before the Bill proceeded from the Commons to the Lords, and this gave shareholders the opportunity to discuss the question again. Once more the Chairman explained the background and made the points that the line had already been before Parliament, that there was now a large amount of ironstone traffic to be expected, and that there was considerable local interest in obtaining the line. A Mr Grundy from Northampton, speaking for the project, commented that already one establishment in South Wales had contracted for a supply of 1,000 tons a week from the new ironstone field, and he stated that the South Midland project had always [*sic*] been favoured by the landowners of the area.

There was opposition from a regular attender at LNW meetings, a certain Mr Puncher, who thought that it appeared that the Company was paying too much interest to the local inhabitants and not enough to its own finances — especially as Northampton already had railway communication. The Chairman repeated the points of his defence of the scheme, but Mr Puncher, who found a Seconder from amongst the proprietors in the locality, pursued his opposition. General Anson's next comment seems to be a model of obscurantism:

> I have been asked whether I can give additional reasons for urging the adoption of this line upon the meeting. Now, there are always some reasons which it is perhaps best not to urge. The railway interest is still in an unsettled state; we are unsettled in our alliances; it is necessary that we should occupy the country and protect our interests. I would rather not give any further reasons for adopting the proposal. I am satisfied, however, that it is one of which the proprietors will all ultimately approve.[18]

The comment on the protection of interests is highly significant. But Mr Puncher did not yet approve, for it seemed to him that the project was simply to give more accommodation to a town that was already provided for, and he pressed his opposition to a vote, which he lost 45 to 17. However, under the Wharncliffe Order it now became necessary to take a poll, and when Mr Puncher learnt that the Board had been unanimous in backing the scheme he withdrew his amendment and so removed the necessity for the poll to be taken. From this point on there were no more obstacles to be overcome, and the Bill duly proceeded through its remaining stages, receiving the Royal Assent (as did the Leicester & Hitchin Bill) on 4 August 1853, under the title of *The London and North Western Railway (Northampton and Market Harborough, &c. Branches) Act 1853, 16 & 17 Victoria cap. clx.*

There are one or two points of particular interest about the Act, the first of them relating to a clause introduced into railway bills in the course of the 1853 Session. There had been some dispute in the early 1850s as to whether the Act of a Railway Company compelled it to make a line, or whether the powers granted were merely permissive. Could a writ of Mandamus be enforced against a Railway Company, or not? It had been settled that it could not. The position was clearly unsatisfactory, and the Committee on Amalgamations in 1853 felt that the companies whose amalgamations were being held up according to its recommendations should have some protection from unfair opposition arising from other schemes which might be purely blocking proposals, with little chance of ever being built. It proposed that every railway bill promoted by an existing company should have a clause inserted in it prohibiting the payment of any dividend upon the ordinary shares if the line proposed were not completed and opened to traffic within five years. This clause was duly inserted into the Bill for the Northampton & Market Harborough line, as it was into other Bills which came relatively late in the Session before the legislature.

Other clauses authorized the Company to construct no less than ten level crossings on this short line and required the erection of stations or lodges at each of them. The number of level crossings is another clear indication that the line was basically being kept as close to the natural ground level as possible. An interesting, and slightly unusual, clause provided that the Company might deviate from or alter the two tunnels within the authorized limits of deviation if permitted by a certificate of the Board of Trade. This was in effect an extension of the powers given by the 1845 *Railway Clauses Consolidation Act*, and its appearance may well suggest early plans for saving on the cost of construction of the line. Two clauses gave special protection to lands held by the Vicar of Dallington, and there were provisions in the usual form for the protection of the Grand Junction Canal and the rights of the Commissioners appointed under the *Nene Drainage Act* of 1852.

A further provision concerns one item of contention in Northampton itself. The town was basically in favour of the railway, and the townsmen had unanimously resolved to support the proposal at a meeting on 23 November 1852. At that meeting some people had expressed the view that it would be wise to try to ensure the provision of better services rather than simply rely on the good-will of the railway company. The wording of the newspaper report is of interest in the light of the work of Joan Wake and Victor Hatley: 'Northampton, it is alleged, has serious grounds of complaint against the Company, whilst it is now satisfactorily proved that the Company has none against Northampton.'[19] But the general view was that the town should not seek to impose conditions on the railway, and the report concluded with an expression of a hope 'to find the Company meeting the reasonable requirements of the town in a spirit of cordiality worthy of the magnanimity displayed on Tuesday evening.' However, when the Improvement Commissioners and the Town Council came to look at the matter, they felt that there was one area where local interests did require specific protection: the original plan of the line involved a level crossing just to the east of the existing West Bridge. Earl Spencer had been opposed to this, and so were the Commissioners. The existing bridge was narrow and in a poor state of repair, and it would certainly need a good deal of money spending on it within a few years. A level crossing adjacent to this bridge on a busy road would be undesirable, and it seemed that there was a chance to solve both problems together. The Earl was prepared to contribute £1,000 towards a new bridge over river and railway. After much debate, it was agreed that the Council should also contribute £1,000 if the new bridge were to be thirty feet wide, or £1,500 if it were built thirty-five feet wide.[20]

Preparations had been made to petition against the Bill, but in the end agreement was reached with the Company and on 29 April a Petition went to the Commons jointly from the Company and the Mayor, Aldermen, and Burgesses of Northampton. This sought to permit the insertion of a clause providing for the building of the bridge instead of the level crossing and giving the Council powers to make a contribution not exceeding £1,500 (subject to a sealed agreement being made with the Company) and to raise money for the purpose. It was referred to the Examiners, who reported that it did not comply with Standing Orders. Nevertheless, on 6 May the Committee on Standing Orders gave dispensation and the House agreed to instruct the Committee on the Bill to take account of the Petition. The new clause was adopted, and it passed into law, providing for a new bridge to be built in place of one that was 'narrow and inconvenient, and might with great advantage to the public be improved' and giving the necessary powers for making an agreement and raising the money. Thus this Railway Act actually confers powers for borrowing money on the Northampton Corporation.

All the works authorized by the Act were to be completed within five years, which was a normal period to be allowed for the building of a line. The provision was now, of course, reinforced by the new penal clause. The same period was also to be allowed for the purchase of land. Most railway acts allow a significantly shorter period of time for land-acquisition than they do for the actual construction, and it is a little unusual in this Act that the two periods are co-terminous. Finally, the Act did not provide for any additional capital to be raised to meet the cost of construction. Instead, the Company was permitted to use for building the line any money that it had in hand together with any money which it had power to raise under existing Acts but which was not needed for the purposes for which it had been authorized. Other LNW Acts for new lines of 1853 also provide for the financing of the lines they authorize in the same manner.

There is a final comment on the whole business of the promotion. An editorial in the *Railway Times* for 29 October 1853 notes with pleasure the existence of reports suggesting that the offensive schemes of the last Session will not be carried out, and says particularly of the LNW:

> The directors have, it seems, so far seen the error of their ways as to acknowledge that the Northampton and Market-Harborough line is utterly useless; and we believe they have so far made this admission known to other parties, as to make offer to the Midland to abandon the Northampton scheme on condition that the Leicester and Hitchin is not proceeded with.

However, a little later the same editorial makes it quite clear that there has been no information from Derby on the subject — and as we know from Midland records, that company had no intention at all of dropping its Hitchin scheme, despite the noisy opposition of certain shareholders and the difficulties of building the line within a reasonable budget.

REFERENCES

1   *Railway Times*, 21 February 1852, p. 197
2   RAIL 491/16 Minute 2835
3   *Railway Times*, 21 August 1852, p. 840
4   RAIL 1110/329, Report for the Half Year to 30 June 1852
5   RAIL 491/16 Minute 3046
6   RAIL 491/16 Minute 2858A
7   RAIL 410/22 Minute 1802, RAIL 410/77 Minute 162, RAIL 491/16 Minutes 2885, 2916
8   RAIL 410/77 Minute 170
9   *ibid.* Minute 238
10 *ibid.* Minute 209
11 RAIL 410/22 Minute 1961
12 *Railway Times*, 26 March 1853, p. 338
13 NRO QS Deposited Plan 66
14 Frederick S. WILLIAMS, *Our Iron Roads*, 3rd edition, Bemrose & Sons, 1883, p. 98
15 *Railway Times*, 30 April 1853, p. 449
16 *ibid.*, 7 May 1853, p. 473
17 *ibid.*, 28 May 1853, p. 558
18 *ibid.*, 2 July 1853, p. 662
19 *Northampton Herald*, 27 November 1852
20 *Northampton Mercury*, 5 February 1853, 16 April 1853, 30 April 1853; *Northampton Herald* 16 April 1853, 30 April 1853.

3

Building the Line

Once the Act had been obtained, the Board of the London & North Western delegated the supervision of the construction of the line to a Committee of Directors. The same Committee also had responsibility for building the branch from Watford to St Albans and for the first widening of the main line itself, from Primrose Hill to Willesden. Later it assumed responsibility for building the Shrewsbury & Crewe line as well.[1] The full Board looked at the outcome of the Parliamentary Session of 1853 at its meeting on 10 September of that year, in an atmosphere of rather more caution than had been evident at the time of the promotions. The Board decided that in the existing state of the money-market it would be expedient to postpone for a time all expenditure not required by special circumstances, and those Directors who had been appointed to superintend the various works were to consider carefully whether any immediate steps needed to be taken, especially in so far as the purchase of land was involved, and also to consider in the anticipation of further authority from the Board the detailed arrangements for each work in order to ensure its systematic and economical construction.[2] The first meeting of the Branch Lines Committee, as the construction committee was called, was seven months later, on 6 April 1854, when the Directors present were Robert Benson, Richard Creed, Sir Charles Douglas, Admiral Moorsom, and Thomas Smith. The appropriate Officers were in attendance: the engineers William Baker and George Parker Bidder, the Secretary Charles Stewart, and the Solicitor Samuel Carter. The Committee read the Board Minute of 10 September to the effect that the new line was to be considered with a view to the cheapest possible construction.[3]

The first action to be taken concerned land purchase: Mr Frederick Wood, a Rugby civil engineer and land agent (best known, perhaps, as the Civil Engineer to the Oxford Canal Company), who had already worked for the London & North Western on the Rugby & Stamford line, was appointed to deal with the necessary purchases for the Northampton & Harborough line. (Very soon afterwards, on 12 July, Wood was appointed Land Agent for the whole Southern Division of the LNW. It was laid down that except where specially directed all agreements for the sale or purchase of land were to pass through his hands.) G. P. Bidder then explained that the works should not require more than two years, and it was resolved to postpone further consideration of construction for a year, and indeed not to proceed with the works at all until agreement had been reached for the purchase of all the necessary land. Meanwhile, plans and drawings were to be prepared over the winter for consideration in the spring.

Various formalities were also settled. There were to be no alterations or additions to the plans except by leave of the construction committee, and no extra works were to be allowed except by authority of what was termed a 'Special Minute' of the Committee. Tenders were to be invited from known responsible contractors, and the contract was to include the delivery of all works complete, including stations and sidings, for a given sum, and also their maintenance for three years. It was to be the contractor's responsibility to find land for temporary purposes, and he was also to supply the Company with a return of all accidents to men. He was indeed to make provision for all sick and hurt men, and he was not to be allowed to operate any beer or provision shops. The men were to be paid every Friday or Saturday at 2 p.m. The contractor in his turn would be paid every two months on the authority of the Engineer's certificate, and if he failed to complete the works on time the certificate would be withheld. Other arrangements were laid down for the Engineer, the Solicitor, and the Land Agent. A junior clerk was to be appointed in the solicitors' office in order to carry out the legal work under the responsibility of Mr Carter, Mr Swift, or Mr Wagstaff (the Partners of the firm that acted for the LNW) as the case might be. The Land Agent, amongst other things, was obliged not to give up any of the surface soil, nor to agree to any planting. All the arrangements suggest a desire for economy and a close control over expenditure, and it may well be that it was at this time that the decision not to build the east curve in Northampton was taken — a decision for which it has not been possible to find any Minute or any abandoning provision in a later LNW Act.

There was a long pause before any more happened, though it is clear that Mr Wood got down to work, for in a report dated 23 January 1855 which went to the Committee on 31 May he stated that the amount of land needed was 167 acres 2 rods and 19 perches, and in a further report of 29 August he said that, with one or two exceptions only, all the land notices had been served. The claims that had been submitted ranged between £225 and £420 per acre. The land was mainly rich pasture and meadow land, and Wood felt that he should be able to obtain most of it in the range of £180 to £220. Some agreements had already been made during the passage of the Bill through Parliament, as was normal: 25 acres were to be bought from Lord Bateman at £280 per acre, 16 acres would come from Mr Henry Holditch Hungerford at £200 per acre plus £2,000 for residential drainage, and there would be 3 acres 32 perches from Earl Spencer at £200 per acre plus, in his case, £1,600 for residential drainage. There had also been an agreement with the Reverend Havilland de Sausmarez for a payment of £5,250 to be made in respect of his newly-erected parsonage. Thus there was a total commitment already of £19,690. The arrangement with de Sausmarez was an interesting one. This particular clergyman was the absentee Rector of the Parish of St Peter — the richest living in Northampton. He had bought part of the Old Orchard of Northampton Castle as a site for a new Rectory in 1852, and the arrangement with the LNW provided for the Company to buy the house and complete it for him, and then rent it back to the Rector for £80 per annum from 1 June 1854 for two years certain. If the tenancy continued after that, the rent was to rise to £100, subject to notice of twelve months on either side. The Company was to be entitled to take part of the grounds at any time at one month's notice if the land were needed for the construction of the railway as long as the land required was not within a set distance of the house on either side. This house was to give the Company a certain amount of concern in later years. On another part of the Old Orchard the original Northampton Castle station was later to be built.

There were other points too in Wood's report. He explained that as the line was to be built mainly on the level of the land few accommodation bridges would be required. Whilst this would clearly lessen the cost of construction it would also tend to increase the cost of land purchase. This was precisely because the line ran through a meadow and pasture area. The existence of the railway would prevent cattle from passing freely over level crossings — as they might over bridges — from one side of the line to the other, and this restriction on free movement could cause considerable inconvenience when animals were cut off from their water-supply. Here is yet another example of the interplay of various factors in the costs of railway building. By keeping the line near ground level there was a saving on earthworks and on works such as bridges and tunnels, and there was also a saving on the land to be purchased, as the further the surface of the rails is from the natural surface of the land the greater is the width of land that must be purchased. But against that must be set the cost of agricultural disruption on account of restriction of access, which might tend to push up the cost of purchase of the land that actually was needed — and this was quite apart from other considerations which could often keep the price for land rather high. There was a further point in Wood's report concerning compliance with the Act: in the Parish of Dallington the railway was to be constructed so as not to take certain lands in the close proximity of the River Nene. But as laid out the line not only took some of the lands in question but also actually touched the river. The parties concerned, for whose protection those particular clauses in the Act had been inserted, required the layout of the line to be altered so as to conform with the Statute.

Also on 29 August the Company Secretary, Charles Stewart, raised a very interesting question, asking whether a deviation might be made at the north end of the line so as to form a junction with the Midland's Leicester & Hitchin line just south of Market Harborough — in other words, to revert pretty well to the proposed junction of the old South Midland scheme. Bidder reported that there would be neither difficulty nor extra expense in making the change, and Stewart was instructed to contact the Midland, with Wood looking into how much land might be needed. However, George Robert Stephenson reported to the meeting on 13 December 1855 that, although the deviation would save about £1,800 on construction costs, the resulting line would be an inferior one. So it was decided to adhere to the original plans. This December meeting also heard that the Board of the LNW had decided to apply to Parliament in the 1856 Session for an Extension of Time for the building of this line and for certain other works on the system. But at a very early stage of the proceedings in 1856 an arrangement was made with the Northampton Corporation and the extension provisions for this line were withdrawn from the Bill.[4]

Surprisingly perhaps, the question of the engineering superintendence had yet to be settled, and not until 10 April 1856 did the Committee deal with the matter. There had been an approach by the Secretary to G. P. Bidder and G. R. Stephenson on 20 June 1855, and on 25 June they had offered to do the work for £6,000. But a report of the Special Committee on Goods Arrangements had recommended on 12 January 1856 that the work should be given to Mr Baker. The Branch Lines Committee decided after discussion that it seemed that Mr Baker had enough duties to keep him occupied, both with the construction of the St Albans line and with the extension of his ordinary responsibilities up the Trent Valley line, and it was felt better to make a special contract with Robert Stephenson's office so that he should be formally responsible for the work, though the individual he selected for the supervision of the works was to be placed in direct communication with the Committee. But pending a decision of the Board on the engineering question the works were not to proceed. Agreement with Robert Stephenson was announced on 2 July. His fee was to be £300 per mile plus 5% of any savings on the construction of the works if the rate per mile were below a certain figure (which was not minuted) for a double line or another figure for a single line. In either case this was to be exclusive of the costs of permanent way and stations. A limit of £6,000 was set on the total payment that might be made, and the arrangement was to cover all forms of engineering charges except for Parliamentary fees. George Robert Stephenson was to be placed in immediate charge of the works. It may be noted that almost exactly two years were now left for the construction of the line within the time allowed by the Act — just the time that Bidder had at first said would be needed.

It is quite clear from the emphasis on saving money, both in the decision at the start that the construction should be the cheapest possible and in the provision of reward for savings in the engineering contract, that the Company was anxious to build this line as cheaply as it possibly could. In May 1856, after the application for an extension of time had been withdrawn from the Company's Bill of that year, advice was taken from counsel as to the precise effect of the penal clause in the authorizing Act, and counsel expressed himself as being in some doubt about this. It was, after all, a completely new situation, and legally untested. At the same time it was decided to apply to the Board of Trade to discover whether that body would object to the opening of branches to passenger traffic if they had been constructed single — a question of considerable interest, as for many years the Board of Trade insisted on regarding a single line as incomplete and requiring an undertaking to be given as to the mode of operation to be employed, even after the Attorney General had given an Opinion on the subject in 1876.[5] Carter took counsel's opinion on whether the obligations of the Act would be satisfied if a single line were built in the case of the Watford & St Albans Branch, and on 31 May the LNW wrote to the Board of Trade 'requesting', in the words of the departmental clerk, 'to be informed whether My Lords will object to the construction of certain Railways with only a single line of Rails'. A significantly unhelpful reply was sent on 5 June 'stating that it is not in their Lordships power to express at present any opinion upon the subject, as regard the Railways mentioned'.[6]

The Northampton & Peterborough line had been built single, but had very soon been doubled, and the section of the Rugby & Stamford line between Rugby and Market Harborough had been laid with only one track, even though all the works had been completed for two tracks. In mid-April 1856 there had already been a decision to lay only a single line of rails on the St Albans branch, although enough land for a double line was to be acquired. It was not long before a similar decision was taken for the Northampton & Harborough line. G. R. Stephenson reported to the Committee on 2 July, immediately after the confirmation of his appointment, that there would be six road bridges over the line, and that of these six one would have to be for double track as it would be at a station. To build the other five for a double line would add only £1,200 to the total cost, and it was Stephenson's recommendation that they too should be built double. At this the Committee resolved that all the works should be constructed for a single line only, except for the six bridges, which should be built for a double line. This may be seen as the formal decision to build a single line, and accordingly to save money still further by bringing into play the clause in the Act permitting alteration to the tunnels, both originally designed to be of 24-foot width for double line. Naturally it was this aspect of the single-line construction that provided the greatest expense when the line came to be doubled not so very many years afterwards.

With all these preliminaries undertaken, the Committee decided to set a completion date for the line of 1 June 1858, and agreed to advertise for tenders. These were opened on 23 July, when it was also agreed to acquire an additional strip of land in Northampton itself for the proposed branch-line station in the town. The Engineer's estimate for the works was £121,580. The tenders that were received shewed a wide range of variation — though it is interesting to note how close the three highest came to the estimate. They were:

George Wythes	£121,266	William Ritson	£102,733
Richard Dunkley	81,637	John Coker	116,504
Treadwell (William?)	122,923	Lee & Savers	108,131
George Boulton	122,184	Pearse & Firbank	97,184
George Thompson & Co	111,429		
Smith & Knight	95,500		
Eastted, Newton & Smith	92,213		

The lowest tenderer, Mr Dunkley, was called in by the Committee and informed of the importance of time in this contract. He was also asked, since this was his first railway contract, whether he had considered fully all the points on which his prices were based. On his assurance that he had indeed done so, he was awarded the contract. Actual construction could now commence.

Richard Dunkley, of Blisworth, was a local man, whereas many of the other contractors who tendered came from much further afield. Dunkley had been an unsuccessful tenderer some years before for the construction of the Northampton station on the Northampton & Peterborough line — the Bridge Street station. He had done other work for the Company, and the question at issue here appears merely to be about the scale of the work to be undertaken in comparison with the sort of job that Dunkley had worked on before.

An interesting suggestion came to the Committee when it met on 9 October 1856 from a Mr Scott, who put up the proposal that the centre section of the line should be built double so as to allow trains to pass, and this was noted. The remark that Stephenson had made earlier about one of the bridges situated at a station having to be wide enough for double track made it clear that there were already to be sidings of some sort at the stations, though the fact that additional platforms were provided as part of the doubling works a few years later suggests that these were not to be loops in the usual sense. At the same time William Baker recommended that the section from the junction with the Blisworth branch as far as the new station that it was proposed to build in Northampton should be made double, and this proposal was referred to Stephenson for costing. On learning that the additional amount would be £2,671 the Committee approved this small section of doubling 'to enable the Line to be properly worked'. Soon after, another small improvement was also allowed, when at a cost of £100 a well-used public footpath at Little Bowden was ordered to be carried under the railway through an archway rather than across it on the level.

It was also in the autumn of 1856 that Northampton demonstrated its continuing interest in the railway, with resolutions passed at a public meeting in the town about the Harborough line being received by the LNW Board at its meeting on 13 September.[7] This meeting had been held on Tuesday, 12 August, in the Guildhall in Northampton, and had been convened by the Mayor at the request of certain of the citizens. The stated object of concern was the fact that it was proposed to lay only a single line, and fears of the long-term inadequacy of what was proposed were expressed, with the sentiment being voiced that capacity problems would prevent such a line ever developing into a main line. Questions were raised about the later cost of doubling if the major engineering works were built for a single track only, and there were questions too about the Agreement that had been made for the replacement of the West Bridge. The possibility of making an approach to the Board of Trade to require the Company to lay two tracks was raised, and Mr A. B. Markham put forward an appropriate resolution. Another question was raised about stations. There had been an understanding that a station would be provided near the West Bridge, but it appeared that the LNW now proposed to use its existing station. Mr Hull, who had been the Surveyor to the Corporation when the plans were drawn up in 1852 and 1853, stated that he at least had been quite clear from the start that there was no intention of building a second station. After a resolution had been put forward, it was agreed that a deputation should go to meet the LNW Board to explain the need for a second station in the town. Some feeling was expressed in the course of the meeting that Northampton had not been as awake as it should have been at the time of the promotion of the railway on the question of a single line or a double line.

The edition of the *Northampton Herald* which contains this report also contains a letter from Mr Markham himself, in which he makes the point that to double a single line would be an expensive undertaking. It was clear that there was no longer a motive for building the railway, and the LNW had attempted either to delay or to escape from its obligations altogether. The proposal to build a single line only shewed clearly that there was no intention of working the traffic through to Leicester and the North, but merely to work a few trains to Harborough just to comply with the Act. But if the line were double, then the northern traffic could be expected to return to its legitimate route through Northampton. It was time to impress on the LNW how badly Northampton had been treated, even though the town produced more than twice as much in revenue than any other *two* stations between London and Birmingham. Markham's letter certainly shews that old feelings of resentment were still very much present. But just below it is another letter, from Edwin Marriott, commenting on the fact that the protest meeting had been attended by less than one hundred people, whose main object had appeared to be an attempt to move the station from Bridge Street to Gold Street rather than really to advance the interests of the town. Marriott asked rather acidly whether the ratepayers were to be expected to meet the costs of the deputation to London. Whichever of the correspondents was right one thing is clear: at least some inhabitants of the town of Northampton were still very much concerned with railway affairs, and were still nursing a sense of grievance against the LNW.

A meeting in April 1857, which was attended by the Resident Engineer, Charles Downes, in place of Stephenson, who was unwell, heard that the works were proceeding as well as the state of the weather permitted, which reminds us of the fact that on the neighbouring Leicester & Hitchin line too the weather was one of the factors that from time to time caused delays to the construction works. In August too it was noted that progress on the works was rather slow, and Dunkley was urged to make more haste. The same meeting heard that the tunnel works at Oxendon (where 'liberal prices' had recently been advertised for brickmakers) had cut off the water to some of the wells in the area, but it appeared that the Company was in no way liable for this. The irate owners had no remedy other than to dig their wells rather deeper!

Problems came with the winter of 1857/58 too, and in January 1858 it was reported that although progress in general was satisfactory, work was behind schedule on the Kelmarsh tunnel. Two months later there was a serious land-slip at the north face of this tunnel, and it was expected that this would delay the work by three or four weeks beyond the contract date. There were other problems at Kelmarsh as well. The work was on Lord Bateman's land, and he had been one of the petitioners against the line. It appears that he was still not altogether happy, despite the Agreement that he had made with the LNW during the passage of the Bill. On 27 February 1858 Mr Rose, of the firm of Baxter, Rose, & Norton, Lord Bateman's solicitors, wrote to Carter, the LNW Solicitor, to state that some of the terms of the Company's Agreement with Lord Bateman over land at Kelmarsh were being violated, and if the violations continued it would be necessary to advise Lord Bateman to terminate the works.[8] The Agreement that had been made precluded the creation of spoil-banks, but as a special concession an arrangement had been made with Mr Dunkley that he should be allowed to make one. The terms regarding this bank had not been adhered to, and a second bank was being built without any authority at all. A schedule of complaints included comment on the spoil-banks and the incomplete fencing (important in a cattle-grazing area), as well as reference to unsatisfactory drainage arrangements. The schedule is also of interest in that it refers to the use of two shafts in the boring of the tunnel. A detailed reply to this set of complaints was drawn up by Downes, whose opinion it was that the objections were so trivial that none of them had been complained of before and that they seemed to be designed to embarrass the Company rather than protect Lord Bateman's interests. Naturally the matter was sorted out in the end.

From 1857 there are two formal reports from George Robert Stephenson, one of 8 May and the other of 3 August — the latter being reproduced in the Half-Yearly Report of the LNW.[9] This was brief and very formal, as would be suitable for presentation to shareholders, and it simply told the reader that about seventeen out of the eighteen miles of fencing had been completed, that considerable progress had been made on the earthworks, with most of the large clay cuttings at the northern end of the line being completed, and that the works for the bridges were in an advanced state. The most extensive of these bridges, the one in Northampton, was finished except for its parapets. Both the tunnels had been commenced, and all arrangements had been made with the contractor for him to proceed vigorously. The earlier report referred to the question of station-siting, and also noted that the contractor was seeking a source of ballast for the line. This latter question was resolved eventually at a meeting of the Committee on 11 February 1858, when Dunkley applied for 5,000 yards from the Welford Pits and for the loan of 30 waggons for about three months. For the Company Henry Woodhouse, the Permanent Way Engineer, explained that there was more ballast at Welford than the LNW itself would need, and so it was resolved to allow Dunkley to purchase some at £250 per acre, the quantity to be marked out by Wood in a postion to be approved by Woodhouse. Another decision taken in late 1857 concerned the manner of joining the rails. In the autumn of 1856 the necessary 80 lb rails had been ordered from the stores, and had been directed to be punched at the ends to allow the then-new practice of fish-jointing if that should later be decided upon. The decision to use fish-plates was taken on 13 November 1857.

There were, of course, still various dealings with the landowners along the route, and the small matters that could be involved are illustrated from dealings with the Hungerford Estate. In October 1856 Wood was told to negotiate for a small amount of land at Maidwell, on this estate, but not to agree to the conditions that the owner wanted to impose concerning the train service to be provided. And in the following October Wood reported that two level crossings on the Hungerford Estate, which would cost £250 to make, might be got rid of for £125, and it was agreed that this should be done. The next meeting heard that Mr Hungerford had raised his price to £150, but a later note makes it unclear as to just what was done. On 11 February 1858 it was reported that Mr Hungerford wanted the £125 for the withdrawal of one level crossing paid directly to him rather than into court in the normal way, and as the matter was unusual the advice of Carter was sought. He recommended that on this occasion the payment might be made without much risk of any future claim, and so accordingly the Committee agreed to make the direct payment requested.

In Northampton itself the new West Bridge over the River Nene and the railway of course involved work being carried out by the Company for the Corporation under the powers of the Act. The Committee heard on 11 September 1857 that this bridge, to which contributions of £1,000 each from the Corporation and from Earl Spencer were due, was complete. However, the question arose as to whether it was expedient to open it before the money due had been paid over, and once again Carter's advice was sought. There was a complication. It was learnt on 9 October that the Corporation would not pay its share until the approach to the bridge had been made according to the plans agreed. Moreover, the bridge had been built to a width of thirty feet, but some members of the Corporation argued that a verbal understanding had been reached after the formal Agreement had been made, to the effect that the width should be increased to thirty-five feet. It will be recalled that this had been a topic of debate in the early months of 1853. Changing the approach would need a small piece of extra land from Sir Arthur Hazlerigg beyond the limits of deviation, and the Committee instructed Wood and Carter to arrange for the necessary purchase at once at a reasonable price. If there were any difficulty, then the usual railway company practice should be followed: powers for compulsory purchase should be taken in the next Session's Bill. In the meanwhile Carter's advice that the opening of the bridge should be postponed was to be followed. On the matter of the width, Stephenson was asked to meet the parties in Northampton and explain the position, and his explanation, whatever it may have been, appears to have been satisfactory, for it was reported to the meeting on 8 January 1858 that the bridge had been opened to the public.

In March 1858 the Board of the London & North Western re-organized certain aspects of the administrative structure of the Company, and one of the steps taken was the abolition of the Branch Lines Committee, its duties being taken over by the Permanent Way Committee.[10] The last meeting of the Branch Lines Committee was on 12 March, and at this meeting Dunkley was instructed to prepare the earthworks for the station sites under the clause in his contract providing for extra quantities. It will be remembered that the Committee had set 1 June 1858 as the completion date for the line, and that the Act specified completion within five years of its passing on 4 August 1853. It is therefore scarcely surprising that on 8 April 1858 the Permanent Way Committee[11] promptly drew Stephenson's attention to the relevant clause in the Act requiring opening by 4 August, and instructed him to ensure that all was ready by that date. A fortnight later the Engineer reported that he had seen Dunkley, who had assured him that everything would be ready for opening by 31 July, and in this expectation the Committee gave orders on 28 May that Stephenson, together with H. P. Bruyeres, the Superintendent of the Line for the Southern Division, and J. E. M'Connell, the Locomotive Superintendent at Wolverton, should inspect the line and report to the next meeting on all the equipment, including the signalling, that would be necessary for the operation of the railway. But there were still worries: on 10 June Stephenson was ordered to postpone the laying of the second track from the junction to the proposed station in Northampton, and the Committee once again impressed upon him the need to open the line by 4 August. On 25 June Stephenson reported that he had examined the line minutely, and he expressed his dissatisfaction with the progress that had been made over the preceding couple of weeks. He stated that he had sent out agents with placards into the surrounding villages to try to get hands, but that if this did not work, then the opening would be in doubt. Summer was, of course, always a difficult period, as much alternative work was available on the land, and this could prove more attractive than railway work. The Contractor on the Leicester & Hitchin line also encountered problems in keeping enough hands at work during the summer period, so Dunkley's problems seem to have been by no means unique. Nevertheless, such news was hardly pleasing to the Committee, which regretted that earlier and more prompt steps had not been taken, especially in the light of the various reminders that had already been given about the date. It was insisted that the line should be ready as promised by 4 August.

On 8 July a further report from Stephenson was read, and details were presented of what had been done since 1 January, what accounts had been paid, and how many men were involved in the works. A report on the signalling from Baker and Bruyeres was presented, and this recommended junction semaphore signals at either end of the line, together with four home signals with 'distant auxiliaries' (as they were called) in each direction for the four intermediate stations that were being built. It was decided to obtain this equipment from Stevens & Co., who supplied a great deal of signalling equipment to the LNW during the 1840s and 1850s, at their last contract price, if they could deliver the equipment in time.[12] And on 23 July a Minute of the Special Committee was read and approved which ordered the provision of a double line from the junction in Market Harborough to the station there.[13] Additional sidings were also to be laid in at Market Harborough.[14] Meanwhile, the formalities were following their course. On 19 June the LNW sent the Railway Department of the Board of Trade the official First Notice of intention to open the line. The Second Notice followed on 23 July, and Colonel Yolland was appointed as the Inspecting Officer.[15] Yolland made his inspection on 3 August. As will be seen, what he found was not to his liking.

REFERENCES

1   RAIL 410/507
2   RAIL 410/22 Minute 2176
3   RAIL 410/507 Minute 3. Where not otherwise indicated, the account of the building of the line is based on the Minutes of this Committee up to the time of its dissolution.
4   *Railway Times*, 7 June 1856, p. 657
5   MT6 157/6
6   MT7 24 Entry 1298
7   *Northampton Herald*, 16 August 1856, also RAIL 410/24 Minute 2885
8   NRO Correspondence YZ 6221-6231
9   RAIL 1008/112 (R424), see also RAIL 1110/279
10 RAIL 410/23 Minutes 3215-3232
11 Where not otherwise indicated, the continuation of the account of the building works is based on the Minutes of the Permanent Way, Works, and Estate Committee for the period 1858-62, RAIL 410/292-5
12 See also Richard D. FOSTER, *A Pictorial Record of L.N.W.R. Signalling*, Oxford Railway Publishing Co., Poole, 1982, p. 8
13 RAIL 410/79 Minute 236
14 *Ibid.* Minute 237
15 MT7 28 Entries 2370 and 3129

4

The New Stations

A main line of railway has the principal function of providing communication between two major centres. Provision of a service to intermediate points is desirable, but not essential if there is an expectation of adequate traffic from the major centres. The theory that a main line should take the easiest and most direct course whether or not that involved missing out intermediate towns was established very early. But any main line would also, of course, provide rail facilities for the area through which it passed, and so would open up that area to railway communication. A branch line was a different matter entirely. This was built specifically to serve a centre — or centres — not on the main line, and here the expected intermediate traffic was of great significance. The siting of the stations was a matter of concern both to the railway, which required to obtain the maximum amount of traffic, and to the townsfolk and landowners who wanted their localities to have the benefits of railway services. All four of the rural stations originally planned for the Northampton & Harborough line are of interest for what they shew of the interaction between a railway company and local interests in the provision of stations on a new line.

The Northampton & Harborough line was built as a branch line, and there is no evidence that any great amount of through traffic was at first envisaged. The question of the stations to be established on this new line seems first to have arisen at the Branch Lines Committee meeting on 14 May 1856, when reports from Stephenson and Wood were read. It was agreed that there should be a station by the turnpike road in Lamport according to the arrangement made with Sir Charles Isham, who was ready to sell the necessary land at half the price of the other land to be taken from him. This was the first example of one of the landowners demonstrating a very practical interest in the location of a station. The Committee limited the amount of land to be used to just two acres, and it also postponed consideration of any other sites. On 2 July the Reverend Charles Frederic Watkins, the Vicar of Brixworth, submitted a map to shew the accommodation that would be given by a station at Brixworth. It was this clergyman who in 1863 opened the Brixworth Old Pits, the first ironstone workings along the line.[1]

Although Watkins's map was examined, it was not until the following spring that the topic came forward again, with letters and a petition being received on 8 April 1857 from Mr Langham and others in favour of siting the Brixworth station not on the road to Spratton, by the Wolfage Bridge, as had been planned, but on the road to Cottesbrooke, by the Hay Bridge. At the same time there was a memorial from Spratton, where land had already been bought at a cost of £300 and where it would be possible for the level-crossing keeper to manage the station, asserting the merits of the Wolfage Bridge site. There was a problem, however, in that the approach road was steep and liable to flooding. Wood recommended that Hay Bridge seemed to him to be the better site, and commented that Langham might be prepared to contribute to the cost. So it was resolved to make the station at the Hay Bridge if Langham would contribute £500 towards the cost and make an exchange of land against that already purchased at the Wolfage Bridge. The same meeting received a memorial from Boughton too. This requested the Company to site the Chapel Brampton station at Brampton Bridge rather than on the Pitsford Road, which was where Earl Spencer wanted it to be. It appeared to the Committee that the latter site would be the more expensive, as the line was in a seventeen-foot cutting at that point. However, if the approach road were improved, then Spencer's preferred site would give the greater general accommodation, and so Wood was instructed to ascertain whether Spencer would be prepared to make such an improvement.

Before the next meeting, which took place on 8 May, Stephenson submitted a written report on the Brixworth situation. Both sites seemed satisfactory for serving Brixworth itself, but the site at the Wolfage Bridge was the better one for Spratton. The roads approaching both locations were steep and irregular, but both had public footpath access. The Hay Bridge site would bring the greater general traffic from the several villages round about. At the Wolfage Bridge the flooding problem appeared to have been exaggerated: only a short length of road leading towards Spratton from a small bridge and brook on the west side of the line was liable to flooding, and even here a raised footpath was always available for pedestrians. The meeting heard that the extra cost of the works that would be involved at the Hay Bridge would be £200, and that the additional house and the wages of the extra porter could be capitalized at £1,200. Once again there were memorials to be read, and it was noted that Langham was now prepared to offer £1,000 together with the difference in the cost of the land. After taking into account not only the greater general convenience of the Hay Bridge site for the several surrounding villages but also the fact that the Company was liable to be called upon at any time to substitute bridges for level crossings at any place, the Committee made its decision in favour of the Hay Bridge site.[2]

With regard to Chapel Brampton, it was reported that Earl Spencer's Agent, Mr John Beasley, would arrange for the road to be improved if the Company would provide the land, and this was agreed on the condition that the Earl should re-imburse the Company for the cost. The next meeting, on 10 July, learnt that Beasley objected to paying for 27 perches of land (which would cost between £27 and £35) for widening the road, and so it was decided that the Company would follow its original plan for a station on the other site, as it was felt to be quite irregular for a railway company to pay for the purchase of land for widening a public highway. This question was taken further, however, and in its Act of 1858 the Company took powers for the compulsory purchase of land in the parish of Pitsford adjoining and on each side of the Brampton to Pitsford road, between the Nene and the approach to the bridge being built for the railway line. This land was largely owned by Richard Vyse and the Feoffees of Humphrey's Charity. On 11 November 1858 the Company acceded to Spencer's request that the road works authorized to the Company by this Act should be carried out at his expense. But this was still not the end of the matter, for on 9 June 1859 the Permanent Way Committee heard that the cost of the land had been £40, and that of the works £639.12.6d. Spencer now wanted the Company to pay half the bill, but this the LNW would not do. At the same time it was reported that Beasley was not satisfied with the flood-water arrangements at Pitsford station, and he was threatening to enforce the arbitration clause in the Agreement that had been made on 10 September 1853 (the original formal Agreement with Earl Spencer). Stephenson felt that what had been provided was adequate, and the matter was left for him to sort out together with Wood and Beasley. The same meeting of 10 July 1857 received a letter from a Mr Luntsbury of Spratton deprecating the removal of the Brixworth station to the Hay Bridge site. It was not possible to please all the people.

Well into the autumn, on 13 November 1857, the drawings for the stations were ordered to be prepared, and a letter was received from Mr Langham asking on which side of the line the Brixworth station would be built and whether the purchase of the land needed from Mr Watkins had been concluded. It was decided that the time had come to apply to him for the £1,000, giving him an undertaking that the station would be built on the land purchased from the Vicar. On 8 January 1858 Wood notified the Committee that Langham had paid the money over, and a month later, on 11 February, the Committee heard from that gentleman once again. Langham was in the process of inheriting his estates, and he was not yet in full possession. The moneys were not available to him to dispose of freely. In December 1857 he had been in touch with his legal adviser, Joseph Tatham of Lincoln's Inn, about the £1,000 he proposed to pay towards the station.[3] Tatham had seen the Master, who had stated that the application for money was a novel one, but that nevertheless he was prepared to consider it. He would have to see the contract to be certain that it was a binding one to compel the building of the station and the provision of a reasonable number of trains to serve it once it was built, and he would also require evidence that the provision of the station would be of benefit to the estate. Tatham wrote that in the first instance it appeared that it was the nature of the contract that was of the greatest importance. If it rested on word of mouth or on an exchange of letters, then it would be necessary to get a new version of it in writing under the Seal of the Company before he could go to see the Master again. He also asked to be sent any documents relating to the arrangement.

Another letter from Tatham to Herbert Langham at Cottesbrooke Hall followed on 14 January 1858, and this started by mentioning routine matters connected with the distribution of the property of the late Lady Langham. It went on to say that the Master appeared inclined to sanction payment of the £1,000 out of what was described as the railway money in which the next of kin had an interest, subject to one or two minor provisions. The Master could see no other way of obtaining the Court's sanction for payment of the money, and in any case, he was not prepared to proceed without the evidence of a binding contract and of benefit to the estate. Tatham thought that the expenses of his appearance before the Master were not likely to be great, and that if the Master's decision were favourable, then it seemed likely that the Lords Justices would permit payment of these expenses themselves out of the estate of the late Sir James Langham. He would send the draft contract when it was ready, but would not proceed further until he had heard from Langham again.

This was the point at which Langham went back to the London & North Western, to inform the Committee that in order to have his payment allowed by the Court of Chancery he would have to have a formal Agreement with the railway, and to let the Committee have his solicitor's draft for such an Agreement. This draft was not acceptable to the Company as it stood, and Carter was instructed to prepare a new one and to deal with the whole matter. A satisfactory conclusion was duly reached. The whole episode with Herbert Langham is an interesting example of the way in which a landowner anxious for the improvement of his estate by the provision of better communication might collaborate with the railway company ever eager to cut the amount of capital it had to expend on the building of a line, especially at a time when money was generally very tight and shareholders at the half-yearly meetings were regularly bemoaning the decline in the levels of dividends from the peaks of earlier years.

The question of the design of the stations also arose at the meeting of 13 November 1857, when Stephenson submitted drawings of second-class stations including living accommodation for the station masters at an estimated cost of £1,000 each, together with plans for a more expansive station in Northampton. Whatever the plans might have been in 1853, it seems that a second station in

Northampton itself was by now considered desirable. Maybe the Board had been moved by the arguments of the deputation from the town in the autumn of 1856. However, by late 1857 the force of those arguments had clearly diminished, for it was very promptly decided not to build this second Northampton station until there had been an opportunity to see whether the traffic required it. It was also felt that consideration of the other stations should be postponed whilst Stpehenson consulted Mr Burgess over the details. Estimated costs came to the last meeting of the Branch Lines Committee, on 12 March 1858, and were for totals of £2,016 at Brixworth, £2,010 at Pitsford (which was the name finally chosen for the station at Chapel Brampton), £1,716 for Kelmarsh (the Arthingworth station), and £4,250 for Lamport, which was to include the provision for cattle traffic that had been applied for by the General Manager, Captain Huish. An extra 3½ acres of land would be needed for this purpose, and they were to be bought from Sir Charles Isham at the low price of £110 per acre. Tenders were to be invited for the buildings by 31 March, the plans and specifications being made available for inspection by Friday, 19 March, in the Engineer's Office.

However, the next day the full LNW Board saw those plans and, considering them to be too expensive, referred them back for re-design in a less costly manner. The matter was raised at the Permanent Way Committee (as successor in this respect to the Branch Lines Committee) on 8 April, when instructions were given that Pitsford station should not exceed £1,000 inclusive of excavations and other preparations for the site, and that the same limit should apply for Brixworth. The limit for Lamport was set at £2,000, and for Kelmarsh at £1,200. It was noted that about an extra acre of land would be needed at Lamport, and that a water supply would also be required. This could come from a nearby reservoir, and instructions were given that an appropriate Agreement should be made with Sir Charles Isham — a matter that took a little time, on account of Sir Charles's absence abroad. On 23 April the amended station plans were considered, and they were referred back to Stephenson for him to arrange for each of them to provide a dwelling for the person in charge, but keeping the total cost within the revised estimate — thus indicating how the first saving had been made! Sites were given final approval, and the earthworks were ordered to be started. On 13 May the revised plans for the four stations were considered and approved, subject to the addition of a third bedroom to each station building. These plans still survive.[4] Stephenson submitted to the meeting Dunkley's tender for the works, which was accepted. The figures involved were:

Pitsford station building	£511 15s 2d	
Platforms etc	491 12s 8d	£931 7s 10d
Brixworth station building	511 15s 2d	
Platforms etc	491 12s 8d	931 7s 10d
Lamport station building	511 15s 2d	
Platforms etc	548 12s 8d	1,060 7s 10d
Kelmarsh station building	511 15s 2d	
Platforms etc	681 15s 1d	1,193 10s 3d
TOTAL		£4,116 13s 9d

and Mr Dunkley, summoned into the Committee's presence, stated that the extra bedroom would not add more than £20 per station to the cost. Stephenson was ordered to add in the provision of a carriage landing at Brixworth.

It is convenient at this point to complete the account of the origin of the stations on the line, since the remaining ones were very soon added, and then there were no further changes, at least to the total number. A significant enlargement of Kelmarsh station was ordered as early as 10 November 1859, and there were some changes at Lamport. Various other small changes took place over the first few years of the line's operational life, mainly in terms of providing the routine facilities to be expected at country stations handling general traffic. One point relating to the line's location in a cattle-grazing area was an instruction to Mr Woodhouse in the autumn of 1862 to put up gates and fencing at Brixworth and Lamport in order to prevent cattle straying onto the line, although the amount of work involved cannot have been great as the total cost was only £9 7s 6d.

A plan of the proposed new station in Northampton was finally submitted by Stephenson on 11 November 1858, at an estimated cost of £612, and it was resolved that Dunkley should build it according to his ruling schedule of prices. Clearly, from the price, it was not to be the expansive establishment once envisaged. Rather the reverse: it would be much simpler than other stations along the line. It had no goods accommodation, and it appears to have been deficient in other ways too, for after the opening of the line the LNW Traffic Committee was very soon noting the insufficient waiting accommodation at the Castle station (as it was very reasonably called). After seeing a report from Stephenson, the Permanent Way Committee resolved to have an awning erected over the platform at a cost not to exceed £60.

It was reported by the South Sub-Committee to the Permanent Way Committee on 1 November 1861 that a horse and carriage landing, together with a siding and an alteration of the cross-over, would be needed at this station at a cost of £364, and Woodhouse was authorized to do the work and charge it to the branch capital account. A fortnight later, further sidings were authorized at a cost of £662 at the request of the Special Committee, also to be charged to the capital account. In December and January minor measures had to be taken to make good damage done to the house occupied by Mr Blake — that built for the Reverend Havilland de Sausmarez — during the alterations to the Castle station. He was to be allowed 40/- for damages to his garden and crops, his water-closet was to be replaced, and a gas-light was to be fixed at the point where he now had to cross the line, the former underground passage from one side of the railway to the other having been stopped up.

The two other stations that were added both appeared early. On 9 February 1863 the principal inhabitants of the parish of Clipston sent a petition to the LNW Board asking for a station to be provided at the gate-house of the level crossing between Arthingworth and Oxendon, half a mile from Oxendon. The petitioners argued that the station at Kelmarsh was four miles away and accessible only by way of a poor road. It was as easy to get to Market Harborough as to Kelmarsh, and from Harborough most London passengers would take the Midland route rather than that of the LNW. Also most goods tended to come via Harborough, as Kelmarsh was nearly useless for the purpose.[5]

Accompanying the petition was a letter from the second signatory (the first being the Rector), John R. Wartnaby, stating that the first dozen names comprised the owners of 2,600 acres of land (in a parish of 2,816 acres), and referring to the fact that there had been some pressure for a station when the line was being built and that this had been dropped only because of the railway company's pledge to Lord Bateman. Wartnaby felt that the time had come for the interests of Clipston to be taken account of. They were: Clipstone & Oxenden (*sic*) was opened to passenger traffic on 1 June 1863. The station was a very simple one,[6] for passenger traffic only. There was no goods service until September 1879. It was also not until 1879, in November, that the spelling of the name was corrected to Clipston & Oxendon, following receipt by the Company of a letter from the Rector pointing out the error.[7]

Spratton inhabitants had not forgotten that 'their' station had been removed to the Hay Bridge site, and they had held a public meeting on 7 March 1859. At this meeting they had decided to send a deputation to the LNW with a petition for a station at the Wolfage Bridge, but they had had no success.[8] In 1863, presumably in the light of Clipston's achievement, they tried again. A memorial was sent to the LNW, and on 14 January 1864 the Company's Traffic Committee noted that whilst Mr Bruyeres did not consider the proposed station necessary, Mr Neele (G.P. Neele—the General Out-Door Superintendent) strongly recommended its establishment. It was decided to put down the simplest possible ballast platform at the least possible expense and to use the level crossing as a station for an experimental period of six months.[9] The General Manager, William Cawkwell, wrote to the Mayor of Northampton on 22 January to say that this experiment would take place, and the station was duly opened on 1 March 1864, with all four passenger trains in each direction calling there.[10] In October the Traffic Committee approved the urgent expenditure of £123 to make the platforms permanent, as the level of traffic was considered sufficient to justify such expenditure,[11] and thus permanent stations existed both at the Hay Bridge site and now at the Wolfage Bridge site too, only a short distance from each other. But the Spratton station never handled goods traffic: Brixworth was too close for there to be any need for additional provision.

One station along the line changed its name in the course of time. Pitsford was ordered to be renamed as Pitsford & Brampton by the Permanent Way Committee on 9 June 1859, and less than a year later it was re-named again. A notice of 5 March 1860 ordered that on and after 1 April Brampton & Pitsford (*sic*) should be re-named Brampton, and instructed station masters to alter tickets accordingly.[12] But there was yet another change in 1881 after the Company received a letter from a Colonel Cooper pointing out that there were already three stations in the country named Brampton. The name adopted was Pitsford & Brampton![13]

There was one significant change to come, and that was the development of the Castle station in Northampton as the principal station of the town, but that forms a part of the later history of major developments on the line.

REFERENCES

1 E. S. TONKS, *The Ironstone Railways and Tramways of the Midlands*, Locomotive Publishing Company, 1961, pp. 48-58
2 The liability arose under clause 7 of the Act, and such a liability was made general by clause 7 of the *Railway Clauses Act 1863*
3 NRO Correspondence L(C) 1309-10, 1359
4 RAIL 410/1042
5 RAIL 410/1541
6 RAIL 410/297 Minute 5613
7 The opening dates and the date of the correction of the spelling are taken from: C.R. CLINKER, *The Railways of Northamptonshire*, published by the author, Rugby, 1960, pp. 13-14
8 *Northampton Mercury*, 12 March 1859
9 RAIL 410/171 Minute 7493
10 *Northampton Herald*, 30 January 1864, 5 March 1864. The issue of 5 March gives the opening date as 'last Tuesday', and this would be 1 March as the paper published on a Saturday. This date seems to be supported by at least one generally reliable LNW source (RAIL410/586 Minute 1185). But Charles Clinker, whose information is normally totally reliable, gives the opening date as 1 February 1864 (*loc. cit.*).
11 RAIL 410/172 Minute 8606
12 RAIL 410/1254 (No. 255)
13 CLINKER, *loc. cit*

Pitsford & Brampton station, shewing the standard building (Douglas Thompson)

Spratton station, the abandoned platforms (Douglas Thompson)

Brixworth station, shewing both the main building and the standard shed for passengers on the opposite platform (Douglas Thompson)

Lamport station (Douglas Thompson)

Kelmarsh station (Douglas Thompson)

*Clipston & Oxendon station - note the closeness of the building to the edge of the platform
(p 67)* (Douglas Thompson)

5

Inspection and Opening

Colonel Yolland came to inspect the new line for the Board of Trade on 3 August 1858, and his report gives a full account of what he found.[1] The line was laid single, with sidings at the junctions and at some of the intermediate stations, but there was enough land for double track and the overbridges had been built double. The total length of the line was 18 miles and 29 chains from its junction with the Northampton & Peterborough line 1,200 yards to the west of the Northampton station (later Northampton Bridge Street) to its junction with the Rugby & Stamford line 700 yards to the south west of Market Harborough station. The gauge was, of course, standard, and where two lines of rails had been laid the space between them was six feet. The total width of the formation was twenty feet. Of the five underbridges three were of brick and two had brick abutments and cast-iron girders, and of the six overbridges three were brick and three had brick abutments and cast-iron girders. There was a wrought-iron bridge across the canal in Northampton of 68-foot span on the skew, and there was upwards of 870 yards run of timber viaduct. The two tunnels on the line had been constructed for a single line only, and they were 518 and 460 yards in length. They were built partly in lime and partly in cement, and they appeared to have been substantially constructed despite the various problems that had been encountered during the building operations. The track was of double-headed 80 lb rails in 21-foot lengths, seated in chairs 35 lb weight and secured by wooden keys. The chairs were fixed to the sleepers by iron spikes and wooden trenails, three to each chair, and the joints between the rails were fished. The sleepers were of creosoted Memel timber and measured 9 ft by 10 in. by 5 in., there being seven of them per rail. The ballast of ironstone, sand, and gravel was stated to be 2 ft in depth. From this description it might seem that the branch had been very well built indeed. But unfortunately the inspection revealed that all was not as it should have been.

There was a sharp curve of 13 chains radius at the junction at the Northampton end of the line. Yolland was using a heavy six-wheeled engine for his inspection in order to be able to test the effect of its weight upon the bridges. As this engine was passing off the curve and onto the canal bridge at a speed of about 6 m/h it mounted the rails and left the track. Its wheels broke through the planking of the bridge, but — fortunately — were then supported by the cross-members. As a result of this rather untoward event the remainder of the inspection had to be carried out using the contractor's engine, but the weight of this was not sufficient to test the bridges and viaducts. Yolland found that there was an unauthorized level crossing at 9 miles 45 chains from the zero-point on the Blisworth line, over a road stated to be a Parish Road in the particulars that the Resident Engineer had supplied for the inspection. This was an unfenced road passing through fields, and it was said to carry very little traffic. There was another level crossing at 12 miles 20 chains which was authorized in the Act, even though the road crossed was stated to be Private, and despite the fact that this road had every appearance of being a mere footpath it would require to be provided with a keeper's lodge and the appropriate gates since it had been formally authorized. At the two junctions the signalling arrangements were incomplete, and the points and signals required to be arranged so as to work together in order to prevent the signalman from making a dangerous mistake. A little more than a year later Yolland was to make this requirement for proper interlocking a major sticking-point in the authorization of another new line, the Hampstead Junction Railway, and it is very interesting to see him making the point so clearly in his first inspection of the Northampton & Harborough line.[2] Yolland also observed that the facing points ought to have double connecting rods. It must always be borne in mind that for very many years facing points were regarded as a potential hazard, to be avoided wherever possible, and this was the reason for especial attention being given to them. At the Northampton junction the distant signal could not be seen from the signalling stage.

As for the stations, both the buildings and the platforms were incomplete at all four of them (Brampton, Brixworth, Lamport, and Kelmarsh). Here too various signalling works remained unfinished, and at all these stations it would be necessary to bring together the handles for working the distant and the station signals. Clocks would have to be provided at the stations and at the junctions. At Brixworth there was a temporary siding too close to the bridge abutments. Some of the level-crossing gates had not yet been erected, and the lodge for the crossing at 2 miles 30 chains was still not built. Some of the fencing required attention. On the track, many of the spikes and trenails needed adjustment, and the road through the tunnels and over the viaducts was in a rough and crooked state. No turntables had been provided at either end of the line. Yolland had been given to understand that the traffic would be worked between Blisworth and Market Harborough, and neither place possessed a turntable. If the trains were to be worked between Northampton and Market Harborough the arrangements would be unsafe, involving — as the east curve had not been built, it will be recalled — a shunt of 1,200 yards from the Bridge Street station to the junction. Since Yolland thought that the line could not be opened without danger to the travelling public he made a recommendation for a statutory postponement of opening for passenger traffic for one month, and on 4 August his superior, Captain Galton, so ordered.

It seems clear from this report that the line was not complete, and that the Company had invited inspection simply in order to be within the terms of the Act — even though the penalty clause in the Act refers not merely to the completion but also to the opening of the line to public traffic. However, the Board of Trade was clearly prepared to exercise discretion, as there is no mention at any stage of the application of any penalty to the LNW either for its delay in getting the line opened or for its failure to build the authorized east curve in Northampton.

It might have been thought that the Company would have made quite sure that by the time the next inspection came everything would have been put into excellent order, and indeed on 5 August the Permanent Way Committee gave instructions to Stephenson to get on with the necessary work, and also asked Carter to deal with the matter of the unauthorized level crossing. One problem lay, however, in the nature of the powers held by the Board of Trade. It could only postpone the opening of the line for one month at a time, and there had to be a re-inspection to order each further postponement.[3] And one month was not such a long time for so many quite substantial changes and improvements to be made. But that was not all. When Yolland came back on 31 August he found that although much of the work he had pointed out had been duly attended to, there were still other things to be done.[4] The parapet of the canal bridge at its north-west angle was too close to the rails. The wooden viaducts had generally not been satisfactorily completed, and their junction with the earth embankments was not good. On several of them the lines of rails were not centrally placed over the timber baulks, so that in many cases the spikes passed only through the three-inch planking on one side or other of the baulk. The packing of the chairs was very indifferently done, the ballast required attention in some places, and it would be necessary to pay more attention to the drainage of the cuttings. On ground of safety Yolland felt that once again a postponement was necessary, and the order was duly made. The Permanent Way Committee considered this latest report on 9 September, together with a report from Stephenson, who was then instructed to attend to the points raised by the Inspecting Officer. Baker was ordered to see to the installation of turntables at Blisworth and Market Harborough, and he also reported that the signalling work that he had had to deal with had been completed. The Committee decided that when the time came round for Yolland to make his next inspection he should be accompanied by Stephenson, Baker, and Bruyeres.

On 20 September the London & North Western wrote to the Board of Trade once again, undertaking to complete certain works on the line within three months if the Company might be given permission to open the line to passenger traffic,[5] and a week later a letter from Carter to the Board followed, undertaking on behalf of the Company that an application would be made in the next Session of Parliament for powers to build a bridge in place of the level crossing that seemed not to have been authorized, on the presumption that this road was indeed a public carriageway.[6] One of the guarantees that the Company was ready to make concerned the mode of operation proposed for the line. This was to be by Staff-and-Ticket, with one staff for the section from Northampton to Lamport and another for the Lamport to Market Harborough section. According to a report in the *Railway Times* for 5 February 1853 (when the Northampton & Harborough line was only at the promotion stage and still intended to be a double line) the Staff system had at that time only just been introduced on the LNW, and there is no mention in that report of the refinement of the Ticket as mentioned in the September 1858 notice for the new branch line. It seems that experience very soon shewed the problems of working with the Staff alone and led to the early introduction of the Ticket with it as an essential complement.

However, the Board of Trade was not prepared simply to accept the LNW undertakings, and Yolland came back again for another inspection on 1 October.[7] He reported that the line was now in fair working order, with the exception of two of the wooden viaducts, one at 61 chains and the other at 2 miles 43 chains. Both of these were built on the skew with openings of from 20 to 24 feet, and both were not merely unsatisfactory but also unsafe on account of the considerable deflection and the large amount of lateral oscillation they exhibited when traversed sharply by a heavy engine. A third viaduct at 6 miles 3 chains required its roadway properly packing, but this was not nearly as serious a problem as the other two. It seemed that the Resident Engineer had noticed the problem with one of the viaducts since Yolland's last visit, and he had tried to effect a cure by means of drop-bracing, but without success.

Yolland went on in his report to observe that the Directors had authorised Baker, as Engineer of the Southern Section of the LNW, to give an undertaking that turntables would be put in at Blisworth and Market Harborough (which indicates that the work authorized on 9 September had not, in fact, been done) and that a double junction would be put in at Market Harborough within three months. (This particular requirement was not one that appeared in the first set of Requirements issued by the Board of Trade on 29 April 1858, but it was not long before it did become a formal requirement for new lines.) Yolland noted that the Company's Solicitor would be dealing with the matter of the unauthorized level crossing, and then went on to discuss the question of how the branch was to be worked. When he had seen the notice as to the proposed method he had pointed out his objection to the shunting of passenger trains over the 1,200 yards between the

Blisworth & Peterborough line station and the branch junction, which he had assumed would have to take place, as there was no station on the branch. He had been told that the train service would operate between Blisworth and Market Harborough, another station being established in Northampton on the new line. He himself could not envisage two LNW establishments in Northampton, but he pointed out that if such a station were built, then it would need a turntable more than Blisworth — though one was necessary there too. He concluded his report by saying that it was not for him to indicate in what manner the Company should work its traffic but that he had no doubt that the Board of Trade would be satisfied on the question of public safety if the LNW Directors would give an undertaking that no trains would be shunted over those 1,200 yards between the junction and the existing station in Northampton. Owing to the incompleteness of the works Yolland again recommended a one-month delay, and on 2 October the Board of Trade followed his advice and so notified the Company. It must be remembered, of course, that the powers of the Board of Trade related only to passenger traffic, and there is evidence that coal traffic was already being worked over the line.[8] But once again, the Committee's immediate reaction to this latest inspection was to note it, and to receive Stephenson's observations.

The next inspection came on 28 October, and it is unfortunate that the papers relating to this and to subsequent inspections have not been preserved.[9] Yet again, however, Yolland recommended a delay. The Committee met on 11 November and received a report, together with another communication from the Board of Trade to the effect that it would not sanction the opening of any new line of the London & North Western then in course of construction if there were any unauthorized level crossing on that line. There was also a letter from the Reverend Mr Watkins of Brixworth urging the early opening of the line. But it was not such an easy matter. Stephenson's attention was particularly drawn to the remarks Yolland had made about the viaducts, especially his comment, 'It is questionable whether what is now proposed to be done will render them safe.' It was decided that Stephenson should send a drawing of the viaducts as they had been erected to Matthew Lyon, the Director who was the Chairman of the Permanent Way Committee, together with a sketch shewing how it was proposed that they might be strengthened. There was a further point: the Act had provided that any dispute between the Company and the Nene Drainage Commissioners might be taken to arbitration, and such a dispute had arisen and had duly gone to arbitration by Sir John Hawkshaw, who made an award requiring about 300 feet more of viaduct in place of solid embankment in Northampton. The Committee decided that it wished to see a report from Stephenson and Carter stating when they had received the award, what the state of the works was at that time, and what had been done since. As has already been noted, it was at this meeting too that another of Yolland's objections was answered, with the decision being taken to establish a small station at Northampton Castle to serve the branch-line traffic.

The Board of Trade duly appointed Yolland to re-inspect on 17 November, but before this inspection could take place the LNW wrote to Yolland asking if the Company might withdraw the Second (Ten-Day) Notice, and renew it only when it felt that the line was really ready for re-inspection. Yolland passed this letter on to the Board of Trade on 24 November, and the suggestion was accepted. The Permanent Way Committee learnt what had been done at its meeting on 9 December, when it also heard that Lyon had agreed, after consultations with the Company Chairman, Lord Chandos, to allow the works resulting from the Hawkshaw award to proceed as long as there was no interruption to the transmission of coal along the line. It was after all necessary to begin to get some return on the capital that had been laid out! Stephenson had undertaken to get ahead with the work at once. On 13 January he laid on the table for the Committee plans shewing the progress of the works for lengthening the viaduct, and he stated that if the rate of progress that had been achieved could be sustained, then the work ought to be completed by the end of the month. The Committee authorized the use of two extra pile-driving machines and gave instructions that the contractor should work night and day until the job was completed. Stephenson was to give a full report to the Chairman of the Committee (Matthew Lyon) by the next Saturday. There followed a string of reports from Stephenson, dated 15 January, 20 January, 24 January, and 26 January.[10] The first of these drew attention to the difficulties being faced. The Engineer commented on the inadequate number of men at work on the bridges, but gave it as his opinion that if Dunkley kept all the men on, then all the bridges except for the one at 18½ chains ought to be complete by the end of the month. In the case of that bridge the problems arose from the lack of timber and difficulties with the pile-driving. It would not yet be advisable to give the Ten-Day Notice. The timber merchants, Messrs Gabriels, had apparently received some twenty to thirty letters of complaint from Mr Dunkley, but they in their turn complained of delays with the creosoters, Messrs Burt & Company. The two firms cannot have tarnished their reputations too greatly, as both of them were suppliers of materials and services for the building of the Great Northern and London & North Western Joint Line in the 1870s. Problems with suppliers, it seems, have a long (if not honourable) history.

However, all difficulties, it is said, come to an end. On 26 January Stephenson was able to report that he had been over all the works and examined carefully the amount still to be done. Notice could now be given to the Board of Trade, but Yolland should be asked to come as late as possible in the period. No time was lost, and notice was given by the Company on 27 January, enclosing the plans of two of the timber bridges. On Monday, 7 February, Yolland made his inspection, in the company of Messrs G. R. Stephenson, Downes, Cawkwell, Baker, Bruyeres, M'Connell, Stevenson, and Dunkley — a daunting array of LNW management.[11] And on 9 February the Board of Trade wrote to the Company to ask if powers for the unauthorized level crossing were to be taken in any of the Company's Bills for the Session. Carter replied to this on 11 February enclosing a copy of the *London and North Western Railway (Denton to Stalybridge) Bill*, into which the relevant clause had been put.

On 15 February the Board of Trade sent an extract from Yolland's report to the Company and — at long last — sanctioned the conditional opening of the line for passenger traffic. The Permanent Way Committee had already heard on 10 February from Stephenson that Yolland had been over the line and had said that he would be recommending that permission to open might be given. In his report Yolland had commented on the fire-risk of the timber viaducts, and had suggested that they might be covered with sheet-iron as a protection. The Committee sought Stephenson's advice on this, and he recommended against taking any action on the grounds that there had been few such fires and that the cost of the work would be high — about £1,000. So nothing was done at this stage, though later events on the LNW proved that the Inspector's remarks had not been so foolish after all. No time was lost in opening the railway, and a passenger service of two trains a day in each direction began to run on 16 February, the day after the Board of Trade sent its official notice. The line was opened without ceremony, which is perhaps not surprising in the light of all the problems encountered. The newspaper report of the opening is more concerned with scenery than with railway matters, though it does mention the considerable accommodation available for coal and cattle traffic at Lamport, the largest station on the line. It also condemns the new service as being useless for London travel! The new station in Northampton itself failed to impress, the comment very much confirming the impression of simple construction gained from the Company's minutes:

> The new Northampton station is a very unassuming edifice, and suggests the idea that it is merely temporary, and that something more imposing will be erected when the traffic is developed. This view of the matter is strengthened by the fact that there is no other station on the new line so thoroughly unornamental.

And as might be expected, there is a comment on the single-line construction:

> The new railway has a single line only. Single lines rarely retain their single blessedness long, and we trust the traffic may, in this instance, be such as speedily to call for a helpmate. No provision, however, has been made for such a contingency. The tunnels and bridges are constructed with reference to a single way, and the work must be done over again whenever a double rail shall be necessary.[12]

These words were to prove prophetic perhaps rather sooner than even the most optimistic commentator could have imagined.

Thus at last the Northampton & Harborough line came into use, quietly and with a very thin service. But the time taken to get this eighteen-mile single line into operation was scarcely very creditable to a company of the size and standing of the London & North Western. It will be recalled that the Midland's Leicester & Hitchin line had been authorized on the same day as the Northampton & Harborough line: 63 miles long, and double track throughout, that had been opened in the spring of 1857!

REFERENCES

1   MT6 17/28
2   MT6 20/13, 26, 35, 44, and 45
3   *Railway Regulation Act 1842*, clause 6
4   MT6 17/48
5   MT7 28 Entry 4087
6   MT6 17/66
7   MT6 17/64
8   RAIL 410/292 Minute 1904
9   The outline of events can be traced from the Company side in the minutes of the Permanent Way Committee and from the Board of Trade side in the Registers of Correspondence for 1858 and 1859, MT7 28 and 30
10 RAIL 410/729
11 *Northampton Mercury,* 12 February 1859
12 *Northampton Mercury,* 19 February 1859

6

Settling in to Service

The Parliamentary estimate for the construction of the line had been £250,000. Expenditure to 30 June 1859 amounted to £62,893 on land, £97,863 on works (including the stations), and £59,407 on other expenses, including the permanent way materials, to give a total of £220,163.[1] The London & North Western accounts shew a further expenditure of £3,048 11s 11d to 31 December 1859, and of £7,886 1s 10d to 30 June 1860, after which the entries are not for the building of the line but rather for the acquisition of extra land and the cost of laying the second track.[2] Thus it appears that the total cost of construction was £231,098 — comfortably within the original estimate, although it has to be remembered that that estimate provided for a double line of rails throughout, for the tunnels to be built for double track, and for the east curve in Northampton. As far as the element of cost for the permanent way is concerned, there is an interesting statement available of the costs of LNW permanent way as used in 1859 shewing the cost of a mile of way as used south of Rugby as being £1,977 18s 4d, the cost of a mile on the main line north of Rugby as £1,915 11s 1d, and the cost elsewhere as £1,867 5s 7d. The Northampton & Harborough line was laid with lighter materials than those here referred to, and so would have cost rather less, but these figures do give a rough indication of the cost of the actual permanent way at the time.[3]

In December 1860 Stephenson suggested to the Permanent Way Committee that the works were so far advanced that the time had come for the Company to take the line formally into its possession and to conclude the contract with Mr Dunkley, subject to his payment to the Company of the amount of money needed to cover those items that were still outstanding. Stephenson and Woodhouse were given instructions to examine the line and submit a report. This they did, recommending the ending of the contract if Dunkley would agree to a deduction of £1,493 from the balance due to him for work already done, the effective date to be 31 December. This recommendation was accepted, with the Company taking over the responsibility for the line as from 1 January 1861. On 12 January Stephenson informed the Committee that the balance due to Dunkley after deduction of the £1,493 was £4,088 6s 4d, and that payment of that sum would finally settle all the contractor's legal claims. Payment was ordered, and so all responsibility for the new railway passed to the LNW itself.

It is not at all possible to be clear about the immediate impact of the line on the Company's revenue account. The only figures that are readily available are those for train mileage, and these can be compared with those for the other recent openings. The line opened in the middle of February 1859, and 2,079 miles were run in that month. In March the figure was 5,103 and in April it was 4,725. Comparable figures for the St Albans line and the Crewe & Shrewsbury line (which must in both cases be corrected for length in order to make a comparison) are:[4]

February -	St Albans line	8,984
	Shrewsbury & Crewe	12,642
March -	St Albans line	10,076
	Shrewsbury & Crewe	14,190
April -	St Albans line	9,410
	Shrewsbury & Crewe	13,255

It is unfortunate that the evidence for the business activities and costs of the various stations for the independent railway companies is so sketchy, thus meaning that it is now almost impossible to make any accurate assessment of the contribution of any single station or group of stations, let alone a line of route, to the revenue of that company as a whole. As Simmons has pointed out, only for the Midland and for the Glasgow & South Western companies do we have good runs of figures, and then only from the 1870s. For other companies and other times the evidence is depressingly sporadic and slight.[5]

Now that the town of Northampton had acquired its branch line, it does not appear to have been altogether happy. The LNW Special Committee received a letter from Lord Henley at its meeting on 21 July 1859 in which he suggested the building of a loop line from Roade to Weedon so as to place Northampton on a main line. This he saw as a way of bringing about the withdrawal of support in Northampton for the scheme for a Northampton & Bedford Railway that was being promoted.[6] In fact, the LNW had taken powers in 1846 for the building of a short line from Weedon to Hardingstone along the valley of the Nene, but the powers had been allowed to lapse without anything having been built.[7] In any case, such a line would not have put Northampton on a through route but would have been in effect a long north-to-east curve to the Peterborough line. Also in the summer of 1859 there were local complaints about the level crossings in the town, especially about the one over the Towcester Road by Bridge Street station.[8] A crossing in the immediate vicinity of a station was always a fruitful source of complaint on account of the need to open and close the gates not merely for regular trains but also to allow shunting movements — inevitable at a station — to be made.

Matters culminated in the holding of a Public Meeting in the Town Hall on 11 October,[9] chaired by the Mayor, and this received a report from the town's Committee on Railway Traffic (together with a number of resolutions arising from a meeting that had been held in Newport Pagnell). It was noted that a significant cause of dissatisfaction was the fact that the Northampton & Harborough line was not open for goods and mineral traffic, and that consequently coal had to be brought to Northampton via Rugby at a higher cost than would be necessary if the direct route were used, and mention was also made of the failure of branch-line trains to make good connections at Market Harborough for the North. It was asserted that the stations at Blisworth and Northampton were a disgrace to the railway. The meeting called for a new main line through the town from Bletchley to Rugby, believing that a branch service was inadequate, and it was resolved that if the LNW would not do anything, then the town would encourage a competing company.[10]

Such news was, of course, unwelcome to the LNW, and various steps were taken. On 10 December 1859 the Board resolved that it would be prepared to double the line if circumstances rendered such work desirable, and on 6 January it was reported to the Special Committee that the Chairman and some colleagues had met the Mayor of Northampton and members of the Corporation, who appeared disposed to withdraw their demand for a loop line if a better service were given and if facilities were provided for bringing coal traffic by the shortest route through Market Harborough. It was arranged that the Chairman should communicate with the Mayor, once Baker, the Engineer, had prepared the necessary plans.

Meanwhile, in early December, there had been further correspondence with Lord Henley, to whom the Chairman had explained his views as to the importance of making good connections from the branch into the Midland fast trains at Market Harborough instead of at Rugby as previously, and in noting this, the Special Committee gave the Chairman authority to enter into the necessary negotiations. It also deplored the fact that the Midland timetable had been changed in such a way as to break a connection with its best service at Rugby.[11]

The same December meeting sent forward to the full Board the recommendation that the line should be doubled when necessary.[12] In the following year there was still more local concern about level crossings, but nothing very much came of this. The reaction to the local pressure for better facilities came in the Half-Yearly Report of February 1860,[13] where it was stated that the increasing trade of Northampton and the importance of giving it every facility had led the Board to decide on the laying of a second line and on the enlargement of the stations at Blisworth and in Northampton. How far traffic had really risen to levels which justified the laying of the extra line and how far this was just a device to keep Northampton quiet must remain a matter of question, but it may be noted that the same Half-Yearly Report also referred to the need to double another single line, the Crewe & Shrewsbury, authorized like the Northampton & Harborough in 1853, where the traffic had already grown to such a level that despite the provision of crossing-places at all possible locations it was no longer possible to operate the traffic without doubling at least half the line. New lines certainly did generate new traffic — if they were in reasonably sensible places! The actual decision to proceed with the doubling of the Northampton & Harborough line was taken on 13 April 1860, when it was resolved that the widening of the line should be put in hand except for the tunnels and the portion of the line between them.[14] What this decision meant, in fact, was the doubling of the single line as far as Lamport, leaving the railway single from there to Market Harborough.

There appears to be no reference in the records, or in the Board of Trade papers, to the laying of a second line from the junction with the Blisworth line through to Castle station, and one can only assume that this work, postponed in the summer of 1858 in the haste to get the line finished, was carried out before Colonel Yolland's final inspection which authorized the opening. Certainly Yolland comments on the line's being single at the time of his first visit. Some doubt, however, is cast on the existence of any double track at the time of the opening in the light of that reference to the provision of an awning for the the platform [singular] at the Castle station in April 1859. However, any new work to be used by passenger traffic would have had to be inspected, and the absence of any report does suggest that the work was undertaken before the February 1859 inspection.

The next section to be doubled, and the first after the decision of April 1860, was from the north end of the station at 62 chains to the Nene viaduct at 2 miles 37 chains, and this was inspected by Captain Rich on 28 September 1861.[15] There were no fewer than five viaducts on this short section, the first being the one immediately north of the station at 62 chains. The Company proposed to extend these viaducts in order to do away with the old wooden ones, and of course it would not have been possible to use the old line whilst this work was in progress. So Rich had agreed to the temporary use of the new line as a single line. The replacement of the viaducts was in line with Company policy. The Proprietors' Meeting in February 1859 had heard that on 21 September 1858 the timber viaduct 150 yards long carrying the Trent Valley line over the River Penk and the Trent & Mersey Canal had been destroyed by fire, causing a complete interruption of the main line for fifteen days.[16] The estimated cost of replacing this viaduct in timber had been £5,800, and the cost of a new viaduct with brick piers and wrought iron girders was put at £10,000. The latter design had been chosen. Although timber had been largely used in the construction of viaducts on the branch lines, it was said, there was by then no timber structure of importance on any of the lines of the Company. The timing of this episode explains Yolland's comment on the fire-risk of timber viaducts at the time of his inspection, and makes Stephenson's attitude to the risk rather surprising. But to return to 1861: Rich had only one minor objection to what he saw, and this was at once attended to.

It was not very long before the next section was ready, and on 16 April 1862 Captain Tyler inspected the new line from 2 miles 37 chains to 10 miles 25 chains,[17] reporting that subtantial brick and iron structures had been used alongside the wooden viaducts on which the old line was carried. He did not like the way in which certain of the girders had been drilled, and he recommended that the arrangement should be avoided in the future. However, for this line he was prepared to sanction what had been done, as he felt that the girders were of ample strength. Opening was allowed. And that was to be the limit of doubling for another sixteen years. All this work was carried out by Dunkley, whose account for the two sections doubled was for £30,528 15s 5d. This account included figures for the provision of platforms at Brixworth and Brampton (which suggests that originally only Lamport had had a second platform), and also gave individual prices for the bridges involved in the work. The two most expensive were that at 62 chains, costing £7,110 17s 0d, and that at 2 miles 37 chains, at £4,134 8s 11d. The fact that the bridge at 62 chains was the first listed suggests that doubling work had already been completed as far as the Castle station — adding further to the puzzle as to when this job was done.[18]

It has already been noted that whereas all the country stations at first provided on the Northampton & Harborough line dealt with both passenger and goods traffic (and indeed were significantly extended soon after the opening), the Castle station in Northampton was a very small affair handling passenger traffic only, the goods service being provided, as it always had been, at Bridge Street. It has also been noted that coal traffic began to be moved over the new line at an early date, and in November 1859 the Special Committee read a report from David Stevenson, the Goods Traffic Manager at Camden, on the effects of this,[19] and resolved that such traffic should be worked by the shortest route and that the necessary track alterations at Northampton should be made. The General Manager's attention was called to the expediency of facilitating exchange with the Midland at Market Harborough. At the beginning of 1860, as part of the response to the pressure from Northampton, it was decided to establish a second coal wharf for the town, at the Castle station, and 2 acres 32 perches of land were ordered to be bought from Sir Arthur Hazlerigg for £1,100, subject to the consent of the Nene Commissioners for a bridge over the river to gain access to the land. Consent was duly given, and the purchase of the land was completed. Tenders for the bridge and for an approach to the coal wharf at the Castle station were opened on 12 April 1860, the Engineer's estimate for the work being £2,700. The lowest tenderer was once again Mr Dunkley, and his figure was £2,293 7s 5d. This was accepted. (The highest tender for these works was £3,454 14s 11d.) It is quite clear from this and from his employment on the doubling that the Company had no reservations about continuing to deal with Richard Dunkley, despite the delays there had been in getting the line ready for traffic in the latter part of 1858 and the first weeks of 1859. Such a view appears to be confirmed by events of April 1861, when Baker was asked to supply the Permanent Way Committee with an estimate of costs at the level of the day for proposed additions to the iron bridge over the Nene, together with a statement of Dunkley's prices at his ruling schedule if the job were to be given to him. Although the price of the day was put at £3,125 1s 6d and Dunkley's price was higher, at £3,299 18s 6d, it was resolved to employ Dunkley and pay him at his schedule.

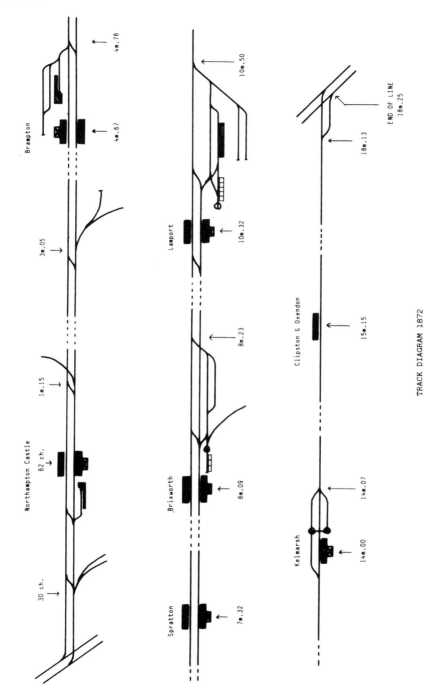

Brampton

4m.78

4m.67

Northampton Castle

3m.05

1m.15

62 ch.

30 ch.

Lamport

10m.50

10m.32

Brixworth

8m.23

8m.09

Spratton

7m.32

Clipston & Oxendon

END OF LINE
18m.25

18m.13

15m.15

Kelmarsh

14m.07

14m.00

TRACK DIAGRAM 1872

At the same time Wood reported the purchase of a small piece of land, of only 3 rods and 1 perch, for this new Nene viaduct from the Reverend Fiennes Samuel Trotman (the Vicar of Dallington) and others for the sum of £208. Relations with the town continued for the moment to be smooth, and on 22 June it was noted that the Traffic Committee had recommended the abolition of two of the vexatious level crossings by the substitution of bridges at a cost of £10,000. Baker was instructed to draw up the necessary plans. On 9 August the Permanent Way Committee received a letter from John Becke, a Northampton Solicitor and the Coroner for the town, suggesting that the site of the new coal wharf might be reconsidered. A memorial was tabled. Baker was then asked to communicate directly with Becke about the latter's proposal, with which he had sent a plan, for a station on Trotman's land. The question was examined further, and on 1 September Wood reported that the Dallington Estate would sell such land as was required for £400 if the Company would then permit the use of points to allow coal and other traffic to reach the Estate's proposed wharf on the east side of the line. William Cawkwell, Mark Huish's successor as General Manager of the LNW, explained that the Company's proposed wharf was for coal traffic only, and made it clear that there would be no objection to a similar wharf being provided by the Dallington Estate as long as it too were used for coal only.

At the beginning of 1861 the Corporation began to shew an interest in the railway again, when on 3 January the Town Clerk, John Jeffery, wrote to the LNW to inform the Company that a Committee had been appointed to attend to matters concerning the railway. It was arranged that certain of the LNW Directors should meet the Committee to discuss the second coal wharf (i.e. the one at the Castle station) and the bridge. On 18 March Jeffery wrote again to suggest the following Thursday as a suitable time for the meeting, but it was not until May that any gathering actually took place, and it seems not to have been a very profitable occasion, for the report that came to the Special Committee at its meeting of 17 May recommended not only that all work on the new coal wharf and the link to it from the Harborough line should be suspended but also that negotiations for the bridge should be discontinued and that powers should be sought to stop up the road in question. Meanwhile, the Company's road connecting the two highways should be closed in order to preserve the legal rights. Also, a small amount of land near the Bridge Street station was to be bought from General Bouverie. A further decision arose from the same meeting, although it is very difficult to see how it fitted in with the other business. The house that had been leased to Havilland de Sausmarez was to be let again. So after this no coal wharf was built at the Castle station, and no coal traffic or other goods traffic was to be handled there for another twenty years.

As for the Rectory house, there was an application in May 1861 from a certain Mr J. P. Berry to rent it for conversion into public baths, but the Company was not prepared to agree to this.[20] Two months later an offer of £50 per annum for the house and its adjoining land came from Mr Dunkley and a Mr Jones, but this too was turned down. The house was finally let to Mr Blake, to whom, as has been seen, the Company found itself having to pay compensation for damage done during alterations at the station by the turn of the year. No further occasion for such payment arose, as there was effectively no change made to the Northampton end of the line before the total remodelling of the station in connection with the building of the Roade to Rugby loop line at the end of the 1870s.

As to the train services in the early years, these do not seem to have been especially impressive and do not suggest an enormous amount of traffic waiting to be moved. Before the line to Market Harborough was opened, Northampton was served by five through passenger services in each direction between Blisworth and Peterborough on weekdays only, and by four goods services each way.[21] A cattle train ran from Peterborough to London on Saturdays, and there was a daily coal train from Rugby to Higham Ferrers. These services were supplemented by a number of other workings between Blisworth and Northampton only. This was the state of affairs in January 1857. It has already been noted in passing that the initial passenger service on the new line was of two trains a day in each direction.

Excursion traffic appeared on the new line in the year of its opening, for an LNW handbill[22] advertised an excursion from Market Harborough to London on 7 December 1859 departing at 7.55 a.m. and arriving at Euston at about 11.15 a.m., with the return journey leaving London at 2 p.m. the following day. The purpose of the trip was to visit the London Cattle Show, and the fares were 10/- first class and 5/- in covered carriages. The LNW was running other excursions to the Show from Wellingborough (via Northampton) and from Bedford, and there is a note from the General Manager to the Chairman, Lord Chandos, which makes it clear that these trains were being run in direct competition with the Midland. By June 1861, when there had been time for a regular service to settle down, the passenger service consisted of four trains in each direction per day between Blisworth and Market Harborough, with the first Up train coming through from Stamford and the last Down train going on to that town. Journey-time between Northampton Castle and Market Harborough was about fifty minutes with the four intermediate stops. For comparison, the passenger service at the same period over the Rugby & Stamford line was only three trains per day in each direction.[23] Five years later the LNW Working Timetable still shewed the four daily passenger trains in each direction, together with a daily iron ore train both ways.[24] (It will be recalled that the first iron ore workings had been opened in 1863 at Brixworth by the Vicar, Watkins.) Sundays excepted there was a northbound train of empty coal waggons, and there was a daily empty waggon train from Lamport to Market Harborough. Southbound and Sundays excepted there were two coal workings from Market Harborough which joined at Lamport and ran on to Northampton Bridge Street, the second of them also conveying meat to London from Stamford.

By April 1875, when important new plans were already under way for the line, the service had changed very little.[25] There were still the four weekday passenger services. Northbound there was an empty coal-waggon train from Northampton Bridge Street to Market Harborough except Sundays, and there was a daily coal train from Brixworth to Market Harborough. (This was the return working of the southbound Market Harborough to Brixworth coal train, and it must surely have been an empty waggon service, even though the Working Timetable does not describe it as such.) Southbound there was a daily Birmingham to Peterborough goods, calling for traffic after Market Harborough at Lamport and Brixworth, then Northampton Bridge Street, and also a Sundays excepted Market Harborough to Brixworth coal train, together with a Sundays excepted Market Harborough to Northampton coal. These service patterns confirm clearly that goods traffic was indeed handled in Northampton only at the Bridge Street station as far as the LNW was concerned. After the abandonment of the plans for the 1861 coal wharf nothing more was done, and it seems that the LNW felt reasonably complacent. Indeed, at the 1861 meeting with the Corporation the view had been expressed that the complaints of the inhabitants of the town of Northampton would disappear as soon as the traffic was worked as through traffic to Market Harborough, which would be as soon as the doubling of the line was complete!

REFERENCES

1   RAIL 410/293 Minute 2478 This account of the works continues to be based on the Permanent Way Committee Minutes
2   RAIL 1110/279
3   RAIL 410/1564 (No. 4)
4   RAIL 410/585 Monthly returns on train mileage
5   J. SIMMONS, *The Railway in England and Wales 1830-1914, Volume 1, The System and its Working,* Leicester University Press, 1978, p. 111
6   RAIL 410/79 Minute 1103
7   The London & Birmingham Railway was authorized to build this line under the provisions of 9 & 10 Victoria cap. cccix
8   RAIL 410/79 Minute 927
9   RAIL 410/1564 (No. 5)
10   *Northampton Herald,* 15 October 1859
11   RAIL 410/80 Minutes 1539 and 1573, RAIL 410/81 Minute 3752
12   RAIL 410/80 Minute 1539
13   RAIL 1110/279
14   RAIL 410/80 Minute 1825
15   MT6 24/14
16   RAIL 1110/279
17   MT6 25/41
18   RAIL 410/2032 Folio 354
19   RAIL 410/80 Minute 1376
20   RAIL 410/294 Minute 3880, RAIL 410/295 Minutes 4028, 4354, and 4412
21   RAIL 946/1
22   RAIL 1020/2 (No. 111)
23   *Bradshaw's Railway Guide,* June 1861
24   RAIL 946/2
25   RAIL 946/8

7

'The New and Important Future'

It is hard to see that the Northampton & Harborough line could have had any future other than as a country branch if there had not been the advent of the Great Northern and London & North Western Joint Line and if traffic pressure had not forced the LNW to quadruple its main line over the section between Bletchley and Rugby, and in doing this, to consider ways in which Northampton might be better served. Quadrupling of the main line had begun at the southern end, as has already been noted, at the same time as the Northampton & Harborough line was authorized in 1853. An additional Up line was in use south of Bletchley by 1859, and the fourth (Down) line was provided between London and Bletchley by 1876. In giving evidence on the Bill for the GN & LNW Joint Line in 1874 William Cawkwell stated that his company would soon have its four tracks to Bletchley, and that the remainder of the route to Rugby was under the Directors' consideration, the choice lying between the simple quadrupling of the existing line through Weedon or instead building a railway through Northampton to rejoin the main line further north, so putting the town on the through main line it had wanted for so long.[1]

In the hearing for the unsuccessful Joint Line Bill in 1873 Cawkwell had said that the doubling of the Northampton & Harborough line, together with the provision of four lines southwards to London, would enable the LNW to carry any amount of traffic over its southern section without any inconvenience to its existing services.[2] What was being sought was, of course, access to the coalfields of Nottinghamshire and Yorkshire. From the point of view of the Harborough line what is important about all these manoeuvrings is that the doubling of the remainder of the line would be a necessity, and that Northampton Castle station would replace Bridge Street as the town's principal station. Bridge Street lay on an east/west axis, whereas Castle was on a north/south axis, and therefore much better suited to incorporation into a new through route and development as the main station.

Cawkwell spoke of his Directors' intentions in 1874, but the detailed planning had begun well before that. On 12 August 1872 William Baker had submitted a report to the Board of the LNW arising out of decisions taken at a meeting of the Special Committee as far back as December 1871.[3] Baker had had sections taken between Bletchley and Rugby, and he reported that it would not be possible to take a line through Northampton with gradients better than 1:200 except at the cost of extremely heavy works. Whatever George Stephenson's intentions might have been, Baker wrote, 'as to taking the London & Birmingham Railway through this Town — a subject so often alluded to — the works would have been far too heavy, for him to have adopted a gradient of 1 in 330'. (The ruling gradient of the London & Birmingham had, of course, been set at 1:330 except for the final descent into Euston, and that was at first worked by stationary engines. And that 1:330 was achieved only at the cost of such enormous works as the cuttings at Tring and Roade and the great tunnel at Kilsby.)

Baker based his own estimates for a line through Northampton on a figure of 1:200 — the figure adopted for the Great Northern main line in the late 1840s and used as the ruling gradient in the Up direction for the new Midland lines built with goods traffic in mind in the late 1870s. There seemed to be two basic possibilities for reaching Northampton, and two for leaving it and rejoining the old main line at Rugby. South of Northampton a new line of $19\frac{7}{8}$ miles might be built from Bletchley and through Newport Pagnell, involving a tunnel three quarters of a mile in length and other works of a greater magnitude than those on the existing line. Alternatively, it would be possible to widen the existing railway from Bletchley to Roade Cutting and then take a new line from there into Northampton, involving what Baker described as ordinary works only. Such a line would have the advantage of utilizing the favourable gradients of the old line for the greatest possible distance (thus keeping down operational costs), and its distance of $19\frac{3}{4}$ miles from Bletchley would be almost identical with that of a line through Newport Pagnell. About half a mile might be saved by building two half-mile tunnels instead of just the one that would be necessary in any case, but the extra expense would probably not be worthwhile. Either line would go to the Castle station in Northampton, from which point the new route would make use of several miles of the Harborough branch.

There were, according to Baker, two possible routes north of Northampton, and both involved running over four miles of the Harborough line to a junction at Brampton. From such a junction a line could be taken to a point on the main line a mile south of Rugby station. The total distance would be $19\frac{5}{8}$ miles, with $14\frac{5}{8}$ miles of new construction and one mile of quadrupling of the main line at the approach to Rugby station. Alternatively, it would be possible to run from the same point on the Harborough line to a junction with the Rugby & Stamford line some five miles to the east of Rugby, to give a total distance of about $21\frac{1}{2}$ miles, with $12\frac{1}{2}$ miles of new line and five miles of very simple doubling of the Rugby & Stamford line (which, it will be recalled, had been built for two tracks even though only one had been laid as far as Market Harborough). South of Northampton Baker did not consider that the extra cost of £124,500 that would be incurred by serving Newport Pagnell would be justified, as that town already had satisfactory railway communication, and so he recommended to the Board the route from Roade, either with or without the second half-mile tunnel. The unavoidable tunnel was, of course, that under Hunsbury Hill. Mention of a possible second tunnel combined with a small saving in distance suggests that Baker had in mind a line that would run closer to Collingtree than to Milton Malsor, and thus would have been more direct from the point of junction to Northampton than the line involving just the one tunnel. If this was the case, then the proposal would have been almost identical to that of Francis Giles of 1836/7, though Baker's line would have been at a lower level and with steeper gradients. The point of junction that Baker proposed to use in either case was effectively the same as that chosen by Giles. To the north of Northampton Baker was in favour of making the line that would take the more direct course to Rugby. The total cost of the scheme would be £686,000. These were the proposals that were finally to give Northampton its place on just such a through loop as had been sought by Lord Henley and by the Committee on Railway Traffic thirteen years previously. A necessary consequence would be a change of the status of the Castle station from a stopping-place on a relatively insignificant branch into the principal station of the town, in place of Bridge Street.

The LNW presented a Bill to Parliament in the 1875 Session seeking authority for the widening of the main line from Bletchley to Roade together with the new lines from Roade to Northampton and from Kingsthorpe (which had finally been selected as the junction point) to Rugby. Included in the Bill was an application for powers for an east curve in Northampton from the Harborough line to Bridge Street — the east curve that had been authorized in 1853 but never built. Petitions against the Bill came from the East & West Junction Railway, which feared that the diminished status to be expected for Blisworth would affect its traffic, from Earl Cowper, Lords Henley and Bessborough, Mr J. A. S. Bouverie, the Grand Junction Canal, the Northampton Coal Iron and Wagon Company, and the Newport Pagnell Railway.[4] The objections were met as usual by inserting various protecting clauses into the Bill, and in due course the Act was obtained, as *The London and North-Western Railway (Bletchley, Northampton, and Rugby) Act 1875, 38 & 39 Victoria cap. cii.*

Within the town of Northampton there was to be a significant deviation of the canal in order to obtain a better crossing for the east curve, although to obtain the necessary clearance over the water it was still necessary to make use of gradients as steep as 1:85 and 1:60. It was also necessary, of course, to obtain additional land at the Castle station for the expansion of the passenger facilities and for the provision for the first time of goods facilities. The only way that this could be done, on account of the proximity of the river, was to expand onto the site of the old castle, and on 18 December 1876 the LNW purchased the whole of the castle property from William Walker. The plans that the Company drew up involved the demolition of everything that was left of the castle. There was a petition to try to save at least a portion of the remains, and the Special Committee instructed Francis Stevenson, who succeeded William Baker as the Engineer of the LNW at the beginning of 1879, to communicate with the memorialists.[5] But it was to no avail. The Company's only concession to the town's preservation wishes was to dismantle the old Postern Gate and rebuild it into the boundary wall of the new station, where it may still be seen. A plan in R. M. Serjeantson's book *The Castle of Northampton* shews what was done, and indicates clearly how the Goods Shed at the Castle station now occupies the site of most of the buildings of this once very important castle.[6]

Serjeantson's plan also shews another element of the changes. The River Nene passed under the railway immediately to the north of the Castle station, so that any extension northwards would have had to be on extensive bridging. Extension southwards was not possible very easily because of the West Bridge (though a portion of the new station was to be built south of this bridge). So the LNW proposed to undertake a major diversion of the river, from a point eighty yards north of the West Bridge to the bridge carrying an occupation road over the river some seven hundred yards north of the West Bridge. It proposed to stop up the old course of the river and to take away the viaduct carrying the existing course of the line, replacing it with a solid embankment. The necessary powers were taken by *The London and North Western Railway (Additional Powers) Act 1878, 41 & 42 Victoria cap. clxxxi.*

Quite apart, then, from any other developments, the southern end of the Northampton & Harborough line was very much affected by this decision to carry the main line through Northampton. But mention has already been made of the Great Northern and London & North Western Joint Line. The early 1870s were a period of very great interest in the railway politics of the East Midlands. Landowners' opposition to railway construction in East Leicestershire was finally withdrawn, and indeed the Duke of Rutland, formerly the principal opponent, suddenly found himself (with ironstone on his lands) rather in favour of the establishment of adequate railway communication. Several companies began to draw up their plans for the area, and a great Parliamentary battle was expected. This is not the place to examine this highly-complex question in any detail, but some points must be made, for the Northampton & Harborough line is very much involved in the story.[7] The Manchester, Sheffield & Lincolnshire Railway (later the Great Central), under the guidance of Sir Edward Watkin — who at the time of the promotion of the Northampton & Harborough line had actually been an officer of the LNW — was eager for a route to the South for its coal traffic independent of the Great Northern, and in pursuit of this objective it deposited plans in November 1871 for a line from Worksop south to a junction with the Rugby & Stamford line just north-east of Market Harborough. Since the company was seeking an outlet to the South we may be fairly sure that it envisaged using the LNW Northampton & Harborough line, but by agreement with the Midland, which had proposals for lines from Nottingham to Saxby and from Manton to Rushton ($3\frac{1}{2}$ miles north of Kettering on the main line to St Pancras) to give it an alternative route from the coalfields both to East Anglia and to the South, the MSL scheme was withdrawn before any Parliamentary contest had been entered upon.

Some people closely associated with the Great Northern put forward a scheme for a line from Newark to Leicester, and in February 1872 this proposal was formally adopted by the Great Northern itself. At the same time the Great Northern was holding talks with the LNW about that company's possible interest in the area and the notion that the LNW might in some manner participate in the new line. In the 1872 Session the Great Northern was successful only in part, in that it obtained powers south from Newark only as far as Melton Mowbray, and did not get the access to Leicester, this section being struck out in the Lords largely from deference to the fox-hunting interest, it would appear. The Midland, which in pursuit of its agreement with the MSL had withdrawn its Manton & Rushton line, obtained powers for the Nottingham & Saxby line, though an important little branch that was intended to reach the ironstone deposits at Waltham-on-the-Wolds was deleted.

Naturally the various companies all came back to the fray when the time came in November 1872 to deposit plans for the 1873 Session. The Midland and the MSL put forward a joint scheme for a line which, while running 'from everywhere to everywhere', basically connected Worksop with the Midland main line at Rushton, using very much worse gradients than the Midland's own proposal of the previous year — though they were slightly better than those of the MSL 1871 scheme. The Great Northern proposed a completion of its line from Newark to Leicester, with a branch to Tilton-on-the-Hill, and this year the Great Northern and the LNW jointly proposed an extension of the line south to a junction with the Rugby & Stamford line at Welham. There was a battle royal in the Commons' Committee Room, with the contest between the companies lasting for thirty days — the longest hearing on a railway bill since that for the original London & York line, which had been seventy days. The Midland and MSL scheme was reduced to odd scraps of line of not very much use to anyone and the Midland withdrew from joint activities in this area, obtaining powers in 1874 to complete a loop-line of its own. The MSL did not stray south again for twenty years. For the Great Northern and the LNW the outcome of the Session was better, though it still did not measure up to what the companies wanted. The Great Northern obtained its line into Leicester, together with the branch to Tilton. But the Joint Line with the LNW was rejected.

Much the same plans were brought back to Parliament in the 1874 Session, and this time they were successful. The Great Northern line already authorized was to become joint between the two companies between Bottesford (where it crossed the Grantham & Nottingham line) and Tilton, although the Leicester branch was to remain a purely Great Northern affair. There was to be a joint extension south to the junction with the Rugby & Stamford line at Welham, together with an east-facing connection from Hallaton to Drayton and a better loop from the joint line in the direction of Nottingham for the benefit of the LNW. There was, of course, also an exchange of facilities and an agreement over the routing of certain types of traffic, and under these arrangements the LNW obtained access to Nottingham, to the Great Northern lines into Derbyshire and Staffordshire, and up to the junctions with the Lancashire & Yorkshire and the North Eastern at Askern. Access to Peterborough GN station was also agreed. The Great Northern received powers to run from the

junction at Welham through Market Harborough and on to Northampton, and also from the
junction at Drayton across to Peterborough. There can be no doubt as to which company obtained
the better deal in all this, but all that is for the moment relevant is the impact of the changes on the
Northampton & Harborough line, which was now to be turned from a mere rural branch into a
main line of some considerable importance.

LNW access to its new lines from the South was possible from Rugby or from Northampton, and
the lines from both those places into Market Harborough were single. Since the main reason for the
interest in the Joint Lines was to obtain a greater share of the coal traffic, a heavy flow of which was
to be expected, such single-track bottlenecks were not to be tolerated. On 22 August 1873 the
Special Committee gave instructions for the preparation of Bills and Estimates for the 1874 Session,
and in this work was included the doubling of the Northampton & Harborough line.[8] It will be
remembered that the land had been bought and the formation made for two tracks, even though
only one had been laid. But the two tunnels had most unfortunately been bored for a single track
only, and for this reason it was necessary to obtain further Parliamentary powers. These were duly
granted in *The London and North Western Railway (England and Ireland) Act 1874, 37 & 38 Victoria, cap.
clix*, which authorised a new line one mile and four chains long at Kelmarsh and a new line sixty-
two chains long at Oxendon.

No time was to be lost: as early as 21 August 1874 Baker was instructed to prepare plans for the
tunnels with a view to having the work completed simultaneously with the work on the Great
Northern & LNW Joint Line. The same meeting resolved that the Northampton & Harborough
and the Northampton & Peterborough lines should be worked on the absolute block system.[9] Once
again it was Mr F. Wood who was to negotiate for the necessary land and way-leaves. As has been
remarked, attention had already been directed towards the provision of better facilities in
Northampton. At the northern end of the line it seems to have been in 1875 that the LNW first gave
consideration to the position at Market Harborough, where the tiny two-platform LNW station
was used not merely by traffic on the Rugby & Stamford and Northampton & Harborough
branches, but also by the entire Midland main-line traffic since the London & Bedford line of that
company had been fully opened in 1868. But it was to be ten years before major changes here
provided a fine new station capable of meeting all the traffic demands placed upon it and capable of
segregating the traffic-flows of the two companies. In passing, it is interesting to note that while the
LNW was busy making joint arrangements with the Great Northern there was at least a fleeting
thought given to another idea: that of making the LNW Nuneaton & Leicester line and the
Midland Rugby & Leicester line joint between those two companies.[10] Had anything like this
happened, the future of the railway system in the area might just possibly have worked out rather
differently.

No major problems were encountered in the doubling of the Lamport to Market Harborough
section (and there was no difficulty at all in dealing with the Rugby to Market Harborough line,
where all that was necessary was to lay down the second track), and in his report of 12 August 1878
the Engineer was able to tell shareholders that the tunnels at Kelmarsh and Oxendon had been
completed and that all the other works were also complete and ready to receive the second track. It
is interesting to note that even boring a relatively short tunnel was still quite a time-consuming
exercise: a progress-plan of the Kelmarsh second tunnel shews that work began at the north
heading on 22 May 1876, and that completion was not until 16 February 1878.[11] From G. P. Neele
we learn that the Resident Engineer for the doubling of this line was one of George Findlay's sons,
Findlay himself being at this period Chief Traffic Manager of the LNW (and General Manager in
all but name). In August 1878 the Company approached the Board of Trade for permission to

make various temporary alterations for the track-laying, both on this line and on that from Rugby, and permission was given.[12] The LNW Officers' Meeting on 12 November heard that the work would probably be completed by the spring, but in the event it took a little longer, and it was not until the Officers' Meeting of 19 August 1879 that it could be reported that the widened line had been opened on the 4th of that month, and that the absolute block system had indeed been introduced between Market Harborough and the Boughton Level Crossing near Northampton.[13]

But this bare statement conceals more dramatic events. The LNW had sent in notice of intent to open the line to the Board of Trade on 25 July, stating that there was a problem: in order for the work to be complete for its inspection, it must necessarily be brought into use prior to that inspection so that all the necessary signalling alterations and so on might be made. This seemed reasonable enough, and the Board of Trade gave its approval. On 14 August the Company sent in the Ten-Day Notice, stating that the line had been opened to traffic on 4 August, that detailed work had been completed, and that the line might be inspected after 25 August.[14] Accompanying this file is a letter from the LNW Divisional Passenger Superintendent at Euston, Mr E. M. G. Eddy, staying at Cloudsdale's Crown Hotel, Bowness, to Colonel Rich, announcing his absence on leave and stating that he would not be back in London before Thursday, 4 September. He asked if Rich would delay his inspection until his return. It appears that Rich agreed, for he duly made his inspection on 4 September.

What the Inspector found did not entirely satisfy him. He noted — in error, as it turned out — that the station building at Lamport, a very small affair on the old single line, stood only four feet six inches from the edge of the platform, and it seemed to him quite insufficient for the needs of a place where there were so many sidings. He suggested that it should be moved whenever the Company had occasion to make any changes there. More importantly, a new refuge siding had been provided on the Down side with its points close to a public road in such a position that shunting would stop road traffic three times. Rich submitted that a railway company was not entitled to disregard public rights in such a fashion and to cause such inconvenience, and he recommended the removal of the offending siding. At Clipston & Oxendon the platform on the Up side needed to be gravelled in order to make sure that no-one should slip or trip over the curb at the edge, and at the various stations there was a need to provide clocks which could be seen from the railway. To Rich it appeared that the works were incomplete, and on these grounds he recommended that permission to open should not be given. But permission had already been given! Rich had something to say about this. He felt that it was most undesirable to open a second line prior to inspection, and he did not accept the Company's argument about inconvenience. He raised the matter with his senior, Colonel Yolland, who considered the practice to be 'very objectionable'. Needless to say, the copy of the Inspector's report that was sent by the Board of Trade to the Company did not include the sections on rights of way by road or on the Board of Trade's own internal practices!

On 31 October the Board of Trade wrote to the Company again to ask what had been done about the matters raised by the Inspector, and three weeks later the reply was received that the Company would deal with the question of the siding at Lamport, but that it found that there was a problem in that it did not own the necessary land. Rich commented on 26 November that as the siding was at the *south* end of the station it could not be considered to have been sanctioned for opening as part of the widening works (which began at the *north* end of that station). He stated that its removal should be ordered. He also went further, suggesting that a fixed period of time ought to be allowed to any railway company for carrying out the works required by the Inspectors, and he pointed to the long delays in taking any action that had occurred on the LNW at Rugby, where the Company was at this period undertaking major changes. The Board of Trade, however, felt that its formulation 'at once' was satisfactory, as some works required longer than others to carry out, but it agreed that it would seek the opinions of the other inspecting officers. It communicated to the Company Rich's recommendation about the siding, making the point that the Company did now have two lines available at this place rather than just the one. To this the LNW replied on 1 December that at the time of his inspection Rich probably did not know of the important new future for this line, and that the siding was required in order to deal adequately with future traffic.

It was at this stage that the Board of Trade lost patience with the LNW, and retorted sharply that under the terms of the *Railway Clauses Act 1863* the Board was not prepared to sanction the shunting of trains across a public road. The railway company was to remove the siding with the least possible delay. This was on 1 January 1880, and on 5 January the Company wrote back to state that it was in treaty for the extra land that was needed, and that it would proceed at once with a new siding. The work was quickly carried out, and on 1 March the Company announced that the siding at Lamport had been moved to the other side of the public road and that all the other works required had been carried out. It also noted that the minimum distance of the building at Lamport from the rails was ten feet six inches rather than the four feet six inches that Rich had cited.

Rich re-inspected on 6 March. All the work had indeed been done, but clocks were still needed at some of the stations: they had been put at the ends of the signal cabins instead of on the stations, and whilst this was satisfactory at Lamport, it would not be acceptable at Kelmarsh or at Clipston. He also commented on the error in his original report: it was not at Lamport that the building was only four feet six inches from the line but at Clipston. Here the station-house was the old crossing-keeper's lodge, and was on the 'Down' side of the original line. Accordingly, it did not form part of the works inspected, since the widening was on the 'Up' side except at Kelmarsh station. Rich noted that in any case only about 200 passengers a month were booked at Clipston — an interesting figure indeed if it is any measure of the amount of passenger traffic that the way-side stations on this branch-line were generating at the time.

The Joint Line was already in use, the last section, through to Welham, having been opened to goods traffic on 1 November 1879 and to passenger traffic on 15 December.[15] Naturally, service patterns over the Northampton & Harborough line changed considerably, largely because of the heavy flow of LNW coal traffic which came into being. The Working Timetable for July 1883 (See extracts in Appendix B) shews considerable traffic passing over the Northampton & Harborough line to and from Nottingham and Doncaster, though the Great Northern was exercising its Running Powers in respect of one train in each direction only.[16] It is clear that by the operational standards of the day the doubling of the line had been fully justified, and it is also very clear that it was indeed the LNW that was deriving the greater benefit from the Joint Line. The Company established engine sheds at Colwick (the large marshalling yard on the outskirts of Nottingham) and at Doncaster, and in 1904 Welham Sidings were opened at the point where the Joint Line met the Rugby & Peterborough line, additional sidings being provided in Northampton at the same time. On the Northampton & Harborough line itself the heavy coal trains required banking up the grade to Kelmarsh.

The passenger service never came to very much, however. By 1911 there were five stopping trains southbound and four fast services (though three of these had conditional stops), while northbound there were seven stopping services and two fast trains (both with conditional stops). There was still no passenger traffic on Sundays. The best time advertised was twenty-five minutes, in the southbound direction non-stop.[17]

The problem of trying to assess the contribution made by any line to a company's revenues has already been mentioned. In this particular part of the country the existence of the Joint Line does at least provide some sort of indication of what was happening. Because the Joint Line was jointly owned by the Great Northern and the LNW, it was necessary to keep careful account of all money spent and received in order to make proper apportionment between the owners. This was something that had been insisted upon by the Great Northern partner when the opening of the line was in sight, in order that the owners might be able to see how the new line was doing. The LNW had wanted to merge the accounts into those of the parent companies. The Joint Line system was basically a simple one: a main line from Bottesford to Welham, with a long north-west curve to allow the LNW access to Nottingham and a long south-east curve to allow the Great Northern to run over the LNW to Peterborough. The last Capital Account for the line is that for 31 December 1888, shewing each company's contribution as £874,958 11s 7d. The Revenue Account for the same period shews receipts of £56,738 15s and working expenses of £32,375 7s 11d, thus making the LNW half-share of the profit £12,181 13s 7d.[18] Such a profit can have been nothing like sufficient to service the capital employed, and it seems unlikely that the benefit to other parts of the system (i.e. the Northampton & Harborough line and the main line to London) can have been sufficiently great to make up for the shortfall. In the last full year before the First World War the operating ratio of the Joint Line was 60·73, with a distributed profit of £43,879 15s representing a return on capital (as it then stood) of only £2 10s 4d per cent.

Traffic on the Joint Line must have been very similar to that on the Northampton & Harborough line. There was through coal and originating ironstone, and otherwise the traffic on both was the passenger and goods traffic of basically rural lines. Much more capital per mile was employed on the Joint system, but it was divided between two companies. As a result, the LNW figure of just under £900,000 for the 45 miles can be compared quite reasonably with a figure of the order of £365,000 for the 18 miles of the Northampton & Harborough line (with the doubling of section from Lamport to the junction with the Rugby & Stamford line accounting for £73,000 of this[19]). If the financial position of the Joint Line must be considered as suspect, then so too must that of the Northampton & Harborough line, certainly before it became part of the through route from the North and most probably after that as well. If the figure of 200 passengers per month at Clipston is at all representative, it cannot be conceived that there was a massive originating passenger traffic on the line. And as remarked, the goods flow cannot have been so very different from that of the Joint Line itself. It does seem reasonable to doubt whether the building of the line could ever have been justified on straight financial grounds, and whether it ever provided a real return on capital, let alone some profit for the shareholders. Justification in terms of inter-company politics was, of course, an entirely different matter.

REFERENCES

1   RAIL 1066/1099 Question 1518
2   RAIL 1066/1095 Questions 5871-5
3   RAIL 410/62 (No. 94)
4   RAIL 410/2048
5   RAIL 410/112 Minute 45141
6   R. M. SERJEANTSON, *The Castle of Northampton,*
    Joseph Tebbutt, Northampton, 1908, *vide* large plan
7   For a full account of these affairs see: George DOW,
    Great Central, Vol. II, Locomotive Publishing
    Company, 1962; C. H. GRINLING, *The History of the
    Great Northern Railway,* reprinted with additional
    chapters by H. V. Borley and C. Hamilton Ellis,
    George Allen & Unwin, 1966; John WROTTESLEY,
    The Great Northern Railway, Vol II, Batsford, 1979;
    passim
8   RAIL 410/102 Minute 31655
9   RAIL 410/104 Minutes 34405 and 34436
10 RAIL 410/107 Minute 39057
11 NRO Maps 3743
12 MT6 281/7
13 RAIL 410/594 Minute 19963
14 MT6 246/5
15 CLINKER, *op. cit.,* p. 10
16 RAIL 946/10
17 *Bradshaw's Railway Guide,* August 1911
18 RAIL 1110/175
19 RAIL 410/2036 Folio 390

8

Market Harborough and Northampton

As has been indicated, the intermediate stations on the Northampton & Harborough line remained merely branch-line stations. But the stations at either end had a very different history. Market Harborough was a junction with the Midland Railway and effectively the point where the LNW can be regarded as meeting the Joint Line, and Northampton Castle developed from a very simple affair serving branch-line needs only into a major town station as a result of the decision that the quadrupling of the LNW main line should take the form of a loop through Northampton over the section between Roade and Rugby. By any standards, the stations which were developed at the ends of the branch line were considerable establishments.

The first railway to serve Market Harborough was the Rugby & Stamford branch, authorized in 1846 to the London & Birmingham. But before any station had been built the Midland's line from Leicester to Hitchin (with branches) of 1847 had been authorized, and this was also to pass through Market Harborough — or, to be more accurate, through Great Bowden and Little Bowden. It was proposed to make the two stations where the companies would meet (i.e. at Market Harborough, and at Luffenham, where the Rugy & Stamford line was to join the Midland's Syston & Peterborough line) joint between the Midland and the LNW. But the Midland's line was, of course, not built, and so Market Harborough became a purely LNW station and Luffenham remained the property of the Midland alone. The station provided at Harborough was quite a simple one. In 1853 the Midland did finally begin to build the Hitchin line, having taken its new powers, and it proposed not merely to use the LNW station at Market Harborough, but also to run over three quarters of a mile of the LNW line. There was no question of joint ownership this time: the Midland came in as the tenant. The Hitchin line was opened to mineral traffic on 15 April 1857, and from that time onwards there were constant Midland complaints about inadequate facilities and delays at Market Harborough. In 1862 the Midland sought to obtain an independent line at the place (though a crossing of the LNW line on the level would still have been required), but instead came to terms with the LNW and, in its Act of that year, it obtained Parliamentary confirmation of the agreement with that company which had been made on 28 August 1858 for the use of the facilities at Harborough.

The problems, and the complaints, continued over the years, however. Naturally the situation became very much worse with the opening of the London & Bedford line through to St Pancras in 1868, for at that stage all Midland main line traffic began to flow through Market Harborough, abandoning the old main line to Rugby. The tiny station and the common section of track were put under impossible pressures. The two flat junctions, together with a level crossing in Great Bowden, ensured maximum operational difficulty. And then came the Great Northern and LNW Joint Line. It was clear that there would have to be changes.

In the autumn of 1876 both the Midland and the LNW prepared plans for substantial alterations. The Midland had quite a dramatic proposal, involving a major new line which would have brought the town a new and separate station substantially closer to its centre and would have avoided contact with the LNW altogether. The LNW proposed a new line running more or less on the existing route but crossing above the Midland to come down on the west side of the station.[1] Of course the two companies opposed each other's proposals, and nothing was done. In the following year the LNW considered action again, but decided after talking to the Midland to do nothing except acquire land. In 1878 the Company considered the position of a proposed new station, and in July orders were given for the purchase of land in anticipation of a Bill for the following Session. Discussion continued during the summer, and in October steps were taken to consult the Midland to see if it would be prepared to contribute to the changes.

Early in 1879 formal talks were opened, and in January 1880 the Midland instructed its Engineer, John Underwood, to prepare a plan for the proposed new line. The following month the General Manager reported on the state of negotiations with the LNW and was authorized by his Board to continue consultation. Plans resulted, each side having its own ideas to put forward. The LNW accepted alternative plans from Francis Stevenson in March 1880 and ordered a copy to be sent to the Midland, and agreement between the companies was reached on 3 June 1880. At a meeting in London on that day Underwood had suggested that Stevenson's plans should be adopted, but with an alteration of the gradient so the Midland line would need nothing steeper than 1:160, and it was agreed that there should be a joint passenger station but separate goods establishments. A junction for the interchange of traffic was also to be kept. The new lines were to belong to the Midland, the expense being met by that company, subject to agreement on a contribution to be made by the LNW because of the advantage that it would obtain. The LNW was also to buy out the Midland's rights in the existing station.[2] On this basis the companies agreed to go to Parliament in the next Session, and an Act was obtained on 3 June 1881. The actual railway works were estimated to cost £125,512 7s 6d, with the new station costing another £66,000. In addition, two road alterations were required, to cost £7,385 and £7,059 15s respectively.[3]

There appears to have been no great hurry to get on with the work once the Act had been obtained, despite the difficulties of the old station, for it was not until the autumn of 1882, after various minor points had been discussed with the Midland and agreed, that progress could really begin and Francis Stevenson could draw up the contract. The works of the station were to commence on 1 May 1883 and were to be completed by 31 December of that year. Some of the contract drawings survive, but unfortunately they are not signed, and so it cannot be ascertained who was actually responsible for the design of the very attractive Queen Anne style station-house. But it is reasonable to assume that Stevenson acted as his own architect, especially as the station blends into its surroundings so well and it is known that Stevenson had an interest in fitting work into its environment.[4]

The LNW approached the Board of Trade in April 1883 for permission to make various temporary alterations and arrangements to lines and signalling whilst the works were in progress, and approval was given. As far as can be judged, work proceeded smoothly, and it is recorded that the new station was brought into use on 14 September 1884.[5] Work on the new line took longer. The Midland facilities were inspected by Major Marindin in July 1885, and subject to one minor provision about the location of a starting signal he found everything in good order. This was considered as the new pair of lines. The old Great Bowden and Midland junctions were closed and the new connection through the exchange sidings brought into use, together with the new line, on 28 June 1885.[6]

On the LNW side there was more work to be done, for a complete re-design of the whole station area took place, and in addition, as late as November 1885, the Company decided to dispense with the junction of the Rugby and Northampton lines at Little Bowden and to bring the two pairs of tracks independently into the station at a cost of about £3,000, and Mr Hull, the Estate Agent, was given authority to buy extra land if it should be cheaper to widen the embankment rather than build retaining walls.[7] So it was that the final inspection did not take place until 4 September 1886, when General Hutchinson stated that the works had been well carried out and that subject to three minor alterations permission for use might be given.[8] With so much money being spent there is one very small amount that is worth noting: on 6 February 1885 the Midland decided to light its new goods station with gas, the cost of the fittings being put at £120 10s 7d. The Locomotive Committee, which looked after such things, was ordered to have the work carried out.[9]

Market Harborough - the LNW side of the 1884 station, shewing the Up-side bay and the goods lines on the Down side (Douglas Thompson)

The new station had its buildings in the 'V' between the lines of the two companies and was slightly to the south of its predecessor. It was the only example in Leicestershire of a joint station, where the two companies involved shared the expenses of construction and of operation and had a joint say in management. The LNW and the Midland appear to have got on quite well with each other here, at least during the building period, and the management of the station up to Grouping does not seem to have produced any friction between them. The design was a very sensible one, segregating completely the traffic flows of the two companies whilst still providing facilities for exchange. And by the provision of a joint station Market Harborough was enabled to avoid the ridiculous situation so often encountered in Britain of a small town with two (or more) stations physically separated one from the other.

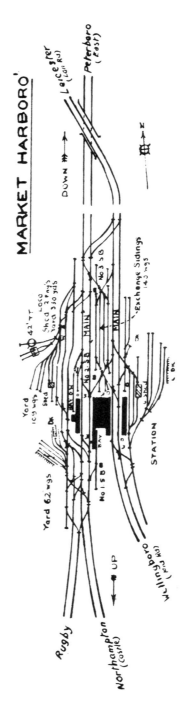

Track diagram 1929 (Leicester University Library)

The position in Northampton was rather different. Market Harborough station, however inadequate, had functioned as a major junction and also as the general railway station for a small town, dealing with all classes of traffic for the two companies. But in Northampton the main station had been Bridge Street, and as has been indicated, the Castle station was a very small affair, handling passenger traffic only, though with its carriage landing facility too. The changes envisaged were very great. There would be a heavy goods traffic, both from the new Joint Line and from the existing main line to which the new loop was to act as a relief, there would be the express passenger services for which Northampton had waited so long, and there would also be all the branch services, for one of the reasons behind the provision of the east curve was a desire to be able to bring the Peterborough trains into the new station when it was available. Two platforms sited on the through lines would certainly not suffice. And of course much more elaborate buildings were going to be needed, to provide the facilities that the travelling public had come to expect from their major stations.

The necessary space had been gained, as has already been seen, by the purchase of the old castle property and by the powers that had been taken in 1878 for the diversion of the river. On 17 January 1879 the Special Committee of the LNW Board approved a plan for the provision of the new passenger facilities at Northampton, at an estimated cost of £30,000.[10] A month later came a minor but very interesting decision, when in response to a report from George Findlay it was decided that it would be desirable to have a standard height of twenty-one inches for the platforms of the new stations being built at Bletchley, Patricroft, and Northampton.

As travellers in Europe will have noticed, platform height is something that can vary very considerably. Britain is unusual in having very high platforms, so that there is no great step upwards to be negotiated in getting into trains, and this helps considerably in speeding up the handling of trains in stations. The Berlin S-Bahn has high platforms for just the same reason, but in general European countries have relatively low platforms, even today, with a consequent need for all to climb up into coaches. There is some evidence that with early German railways platforms were high, but that they diminished as soon as multiple platforms began to appear, in order to ease the problem of access from one platform to another.[11] As for Findlay's twenty-one inches, even that would be low by modern standards. Readers must have noticed that whenever modernization works are undertaken on British Railways they appear to include raising the platforms. This work is necessary because so many stations do in fact have platforms which are below the heights now required by the Department of Transport. The LNW in 1879 was doing its little bit towards standardization!

In July of the same year the Special Committee took the advice of the Hotel Committee and decreed that the Engineer should provide for a Refreshment Room in his plans for the new station. Indeed, in May 1880 there was even thought of a railway hotel, when Stevenson was asked to consider together with Messrs Hull and Taylor whether the existing school building belonging to the Company might be converted into a hotel by adding another storey and extending the basement.[12] There were also some houses to be bought in the vicinity of the station, and in September Wood was instructed to report on progress and John Kellett, the Divisional Engineer, was told to submit a plan for making use of them. On 17 December 1880 Kellett reported back that instead of pulling these houses down he proposed to build the offices that he and Purssell needed in the gardens at the back at a cost of £725, and this was approved subject to ensuring that Cawkwell agreed with what was happening by stipulating that he should sign the plans.[13] (Mr R. Purssell had come to Northampton from Lancaster in November 1879 as the first District Superintendent of the newly-created Northampton District, which had been formed on the opening of the Joint Line from that line, the Northampton & Harborough, the Rugby & Stamford, the Northampton & Peterborough, and the new Seaton & Wansford.)

A true winter's topic was debated by the Special Committee on 21 January 1881, when, rather appropriately, instructions were given for Stevenson and Webb to arrange for the heating of the waiting rooms of the new stations at Northampton, Rugby, Bletchley, Wolverhampton, and Manchester Victoria by hot water pipes.[14] Thus central heating was to replace the traditional open fires — and one must hope that intending passengers were more reliably kept warm! But nine months later the Company declined to follow progress in another area: a letter from Messrs Pressland & Son of Northampton was read at the meeting on 23 September asking whether the Company would adopt electric lighting for the station if this new method of illumination were to be introduced into the town, and the Company declared in response that it was not interested.[15]

The question of engine sheds had been considered in the course of a general discussion of the plans of the station by the Special Committee on 19 May 1880, and various facilities were authorized for the care of carriages in December 1881. Six weeks earlier a plan had been received from Stevenson of a new road that was to be made up by the Corporation at the station, and the Company had agreed to what was being suggested and authorized Mr Hull to settle the land prices.[16] Goods facilities were also considered at the May 1880 meeting, when the relevant plan was given general approval. At the same time Stevenson was given authority to proceed with the widening of the line between the station and the junction with the Rugby line near Brampton (Kingsthorpe Junction) and to build the additional bridge over the Nene that would be necessary.[17] The powers under the 1875 Act provided for the new line from Roade to terminate at the north end of the old station, and for the line to Rugby to begin at Kingsthorpe junction. The resolution to obtain parliamentary authorization for the widening between these two points was taken six months after Stevenson had been instructed to make a beginning, at the Special Committee on 22 October 1880, when it was decided that powers should be sought in the 1881 Bill.[18] By the following November the Committee was ready to sanction the purchase of the necessary additional land and to put in hand the works, which had duly been authorized under the *London and North Western Railway (New Railways) Act 1881, 44 & 45 Victoria cap. cxli*.[19]

Work here seems to have proceeded as smoothly as it did in Market Harborough. The Board of Trade approved a siding for construction access to the Rugby line at Kingsthorpe on 1 July 1878, and on 6 August 1880 it approved the completed east curve.[20] For the major works Rich was appointed the inspector on 23 July 1881, and he made his inspection of the various junctions on 9 August.[21] The report follows the usual form, and its most interesting feature is the plan of Northampton itself that is included. This indicates that the old running lines were to remain as the Up through line in the new arrangement and the Down main line. At the time of the inspection the new Up platform line had not been completed, and neither had the north-end bays. The south-end bays were already in place, and the junction with the new Roade line was, of course, in. As to the actual openings, the east curve was in use for goods by April 1879 according to C. R. Clinker, with its opening for passenger traffic coming on 3 April 1882, when all but one of the Northampton & Peterborough line trains were diverted to Castle.[22] The quadrupling from Bletchley to the new junction at Roade was opened to goods traffic on 1 August 1881 and to passenger trains on 31 July 1882. The new line between Roade and Rugby was also opened to goods traffic on 1 August 1881, with passenger services beginning on the northern section on 1 December of that year, on which date the new Castle passenger station was also opened. Passenger trains began on the southern section on 3 April 1882. LNW sources give the opening of the Castle station to goods traffic as 1 May 1882.[23] The final development was the southern parallel to what had been done at Market

Harborough, the opening of the quadruple track between the station and the junction together with the elimination of the junction. This took place on 3 May 1885, and Rich reported on the removal of the old connections and the satisfactory installation of the new ones on 12 June.[24]

Thus Northampton at last had its loop line, and found itself also on a very important coal artery from Nottingham and the North to Camden. Bridge Street ceased to be a station of any consequence — which is probably why its elegant main building was able to survive almost intact for so long. As far as passenger traffic was concerned, the position of Northampton was certainly much improved. Better services were available to the East Midlands and beyond as a result of the opening of the Joint Line, but much more importantly, completion of the loop to Rugby allowed a number of LNW main-line services to be diverted to serve the town, and a reasonable service of express trains was provided by the LNW until the First World War.

Northampton Castle - the 1881 station looking north (Douglas Thompson)

It will be recalled that a part of the deal which led to the building of the Joint Line was a grant by the LNW of Running Powers to the Great Northern between Welham and Northampton. That company was anxious to exercise those powers as soon as it had the opportunity, and one passenger train in each direction was run between Retford and Northampton from 1 January 1880, to make connections with Great Northern main-line services. The southbound service left the main line at Newark at 9.03 a.m. for Bottesford and the Joint Line, called at Market Harborough at 10.50 a.m., and arrived in Northampton at 11.20 a.m. The northbound train left Northampton at 3.15 p.m., called at Market Harborough at 3.44 p.m., and reached Newark at 5.15 p.m. In both directions between Northampton and Market Harborough the trains called at the intermediate stations only if required to pick up or set down through passengers.[25]

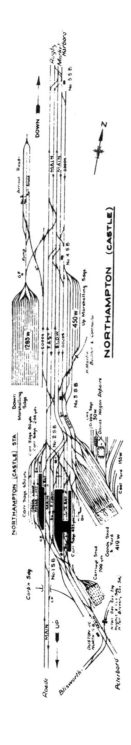

Track diagram 1947, shewing the wartime restoration of the junction at No. 5 box
(Leicester University Library)

Northampton Castle - the 1881 station south bays, now a car park (Douglas Thompson)

Northampton Bridge Street station, the original building (Douglas Thompson)

Mr E. J. Blake, the Secretary of the South Staffordshire and Midland Railway Companies Association, was appointed the Great Northern's Agent in Northampton for goods traffic, at a salary of £300 per annum, and an office was taken in Gold Street for £12 per annum. Soon afterwards, a house was rented at £70 per annum as an office for the Agent. Messrs George Hurst & Son were appointed as carriers. (The intention at first had been to appoint a local coal merchant and carter, Mr Hillyer, for this work.) The goods service began on 1 March 1880. Whether at first the Great Northern ran its own trains is not clear, but certainly by July 1882 the traffic was being worked from Market Harborough on LNW trains.[26] Through working had clearly been envisaged, for a year earlier it had been agreed that if the Great Northern decided to run its own through goods trains the LNW would provide an engine shed and other necessary accommodation. As the newcomer to the district Mr Blake had to win traffic from established routes, and at the beginning of 1882 he was provided by the Company with a horse and dog-cart to enable him to canvass the area more efficiently. Representatives of the other companies were already so provided. Also in 1882 the Great Northern, having taken over its own carting in October 1880, decided to employ an Assistant Clerk and three draymen in Northampton.

There is a conflict of evidence over the advent of the Great Northern. At a meeting at King's Cross on 23 December 1879 Henry Oakley, the Great Northern's General Manager, had said that his company proposed to put on one through service each way as from 1 January. Findlay had explained that this would be difficult on account of the state of the works, and he had asked for a deferral.[27] And the Minutes of the LNW Special Committee of 16 January 1880 record that the Great Northern had given notice of its intention to work traffic as from 2 February. Findlay was given instructions to confer with Oakley about the interim arrangements for working the Great Northern service until the enlarged station was ready.[28] But the Great Northern public timetable, an advertisement in the Northampton press, and a Minute of the LNW Officers' Conference all support 1 January, and so the balance of the evidence does appear to be in favour of this date.

Another matter raised at the Special Committee on 16 January was a request from Oakley for his company's trains to be allowed to carry local passengers between Northampton and Market Harborough, and this was referred to the Chairman and Findlay to deal with.[29] The outcome was an agreement that from 1 February the Great Northern might indeed convey local passengers on the understanding that it should be allowed 15% for working expenses and that the arrangement might be terminated at short notice at any time.[30] In fact, it was some time before advantage was taken of this permission: until the end of October 1881 the Great Northern trains called on their way south to set down only, if required, at the intermediate stations. Going north they called to pick up only. But as from 1 November 1881 their schedules were lengthened in order to accommodate traffic stops at all stations.[31] The service operated to and from Northampton by the Great Northern remained sparse, however. The LNW Working Timetable for 1882 shews two passenger services in each direction, but that for 1883 has just an express service from Nottingham to Northampton at 9.23 a.m., returning at 1 p.m. as a local train. The Great Northern naturally worked its own goods traffic over the Joint Line to and from Market Harborough, and in October 1883 it introduced a return goods service between Peterborough and Market Harborough by way of the LNW line. These trains would, of course, handle traffic for Northampton. The incursions appear to have been relatively minor, however, and it does not seem unreasonable to assert that Northampton Castle remained very much a LNW stronghold.

REFERENCES

1   LRO QS 73/225 and 231
2   RAIL 491/24 Minute 2456
3   RAIL 410/2054
4   RAIL 406/14 See also entry in John MARSHALL, *A Biographical Dictionary of Railway Engineers,* David & Charles, Newton Abbot, 1978
5   J. SIMMONS, 'Railways' in W. G. HOSKINS and R. A. McKINLEY (Eds), *A History of the County of Leicester,* Vol. III, Oxford University Press for the Institute of Historical Research, 1955, pp. 108-28, see p. 120 (This date is not in Stretton's work quoted as the source)
6   RAIL 410/596 Minute 27571
7   RAIL 410/118 Minute 381 Inspection report MT6 389/5
8   MT6 416/1
9   RAIL 491/155 Minute 24162
10 RAIL 410/112 Minute 45128
11 o.V., *Das Deutsche Eisenbahnwesen der Gegenwart,* 2 volumes, Reimar Hobbing, Berlin, 1911, Vol. I, p. 91
12 RAIL 410/113 Minute 47793
13 RAIL 410/114 Minute 49084
14 *ibid.* Minute 49220
15 *ibid.* Minute 50709
16 RAIL 410/113 Minute 47793, RAIL 410/114 Minutes 51230 and 50896
17 RAIL 410/113 Minute 47574
18 *ibid.* Minute 48692
19 RAIL 410/114 Minute 51006
20 MT6 209/16(B) and MT6 255/7
21 MT6 310/10
22 CLINKER, *op. cit.,* p. 3
23 RAIL 1005/260
24 MT6 386/9
25 *Northampton Mercury* 3 January 1880, RAIL 410/594 Minute 20413, RAIL 935/15
26 *Northampton Mercury* 6 March 1880, RAIL 236/147 p. 98, RAIL 946/9
27 RAIL 234/4 Minute 577
28 RAIL 410/113 Minute 47199
29 *ibid.* Minute 47200
30 RAIL 410/594 Minute 20461
31 RAIL 935/16

9

Latter Days, Decline, and Closure

No further significant changes took place except for an increase in the number of sidings in use at Northampton both at the beginning of this century and during the Second World War, together with the addition of a number of connections along the line to serve the ironstone traffic, as for example at Brixworth in 1883.[1] There is a might-have-been: in 1880 the LNW considered seriously the construction of a new line eastwards from Kelmarsh towards Ringstead in order to obtain a share of the ironstone traffic dominated in that area by the Midland.[2] The proposed line would have been fifteen miles long, laid single but with land for a second track, and it would have cost about £350,000. Nothing came of the suggestion, however.

After the Grouping in 1923 the two main routes at Market Harborough came under the control of one company, the newly-formed London, Midland & Scottish Railway, and one of the very early acts of this company was to restore a running junction at Market Harborough. In October 1923 the Board of the Company saw a list of expenditure totalling £14,096,710 which it was suggested should be put in hand following the wishes of the government of the day in order to ease the unemployment situation.[3] In drawing up the list due regard had been given to those proposals that appeared to be of an economic character, and out of the total, general new works amounted to £6,074,000. The Board decided that the works should be pressed ahead fast, and also formally recorded its decision that a press statement should be made — an interesting pointer to the changes that had come about since the last century.

Detailed supervision of the works passed, of course, to other committees. At its meeting on 29 November 1923 the Traffic Committee heard a recommendation from the Chief General Superintendent that in order to develop passenger and goods services it would be advantageous to lay in a junction at Market Harborough between the LNW and the Midland lines, at an estimated cost of £3,575, as part of the new works expenditure authorized by the Board.[4] If this were agreed to, the new junction would allow a through service of passenger trains between Nottingham, Leicester, and Northampton, and also through trains between the former Midland line and Eastbourne, Margate, and Brighton via the LNW — holiday traffic still being of very great importance to the railways in those days before mass road travel, either by car or by coach. Furthermore, congestion at Rugby could be relieved. This is an interesting point, as one of the reasons behind the desire to get rid of the Leicester & Rugby line in the early 1960s was the congestion at the junctions at the north end of Rugby station, especially in the light of the heavier traffic that was to be expected after completion of the Euston-Manchester-Liverpool electrification scheme then under way. The Traffic Committee approved the proposal. However, it had to return to the question in May 1924, when the Chief General Superintendent came back with a request for additional signalling over and above that already authorized. He explained that the traffic to be worked would be both fast and heavy, including a large number of guaranteed excursions to Wembley for the British Empire Exhibition, and he stated that the arrangements he now proposed at a further cost of no less than £3,117 were necessary 'for the satisfactory and expeditious working of the traffic through the junction and on the main lines'. Approval was duly given for these additional works.

Actual construction was dealt with by the Works Committee, and the first reference to the job came in the report on Progress of Works to the March meeting.[5] It was then noted monthly that work continued, and in October it was stated that the installation had been completed. A paragraph reported the installation of the new junction in the *Railway Gazette* for April 1924, stating that the route would be ready for traffic in July, when there was to be a new series of trains connecting Northampton and Leicester.[6] Mention was made of the fact that it had been necessary to lower the LNW track to allow the additional crossovers to be laid in. Completion of this junction meant that it was no longer necessary to run between Northampton and Leicester over the roundabout route through Wellingborough that had so far been required. (This was the traditional Midland route, using running powers over the LNW between Northampton and Wellingborough.) It also allowed Nottingham to Northampton trains to follow the Midland main line and serve some sizeable towns instead of running through the traffic-desert of the Joint Line. However, in LMS years the new connection saw relatively little passenger use, for traditional routings proved then — as now — hard to break.

There had been a very much more interesting possibility for the Northampton & Harborough line. In the early 1890s the Manchester, Sheffield & Lincolnshire Railway was once again casting envious eyes on traffic to the South, and this time its plans were much more grandiose than before. It was aiming to have a route that would place it in a position to compete for the express passenger traffic as well as for the goods traffic. A line was surveyed by Charles Liddell, and it took as direct a course as possible from the end of the existing line at Annesley through the centre of Nottingham and south to Rugby and London. Naturally plans such as these were not welcome to those companies already in the field, but when they realized that outright opposition might very well not succeed, they came up with various ploys to try to make the best of a bad job. One such proposal came from the Midland, to the effect that between Aylestone, just south of Leicester, and Rugby the MSL should not build a new line but should use instead the Midland's Leicester & Rugby line, under-utilized since the opening of the London & Bedford in 1867/8.

Another idea was floated in 1891 by the LNW. This was a plan that the MSL might be given running powers by the LNW (in conjunction with the Great Northern) south over the Joint Line as far as Market Harborough and then on over the Northampton & Harborough line either to Northampton or to Blisworth. From either of these points the MSL might then build itself a short connection to meet the Metropolitan at Aylesbury. Although this scheme clearly stemmed from the wish to try to contain the MSL's ambitions, it does suggest a consciousness of spare capacity on the Joint Line and on the Northampton & Harborough line which might be made to yield some extra revenue. Interestingly, there was no suggestion at all of allowing use of the LNW main line itself southwards from Northampton. Traffic there was presumably quite heavy enough for there to be no question of bringing in a competitor to try to raise earnings. However, the disadvantages of any such plan for the MSL were that the very expensive section of line through the centre of Nottingham would still have had to be built, if such a route were not to be hopelessly roundabout, and also that the poor gradients and bad alignment of the notional route southwards were unsuitable for fast traffic.[7] Lessons had been learnt: Liddell proposed gradients south of Nottingham no worse than 1:176.

The LNW received a letter from the Secretary of the Metropolitan Railway in October 1891 referring to the evidence that George Findlay had given to the Parliamentary committee on the MSL Bill and asking if the LNW would grant the Metropolitan running powers over its lines from Verney Junction (on the Bletchley & Oxford line) through Northampton and Market Harborough and on over the Joint Line to meet the MSL at or near Nottingham. A reply was sent, and in due course another letter came from the Metropolitan regretting the LNW decision. But it remains interesting that the Northampton & Harborough line was considered, however briefly, as a part of a possible London route for the MSL in place of the vastly expensive and unremunerative route to Marylebone so grandly built a few years later. And there remains of course the teasing question that Northampton might just possibly have found itself actually on a main line to London instead of on the LNW loop.

As for passenger services under the LMS, in the summer of 1938, during the glorious evening of the steam railway, the line operated on weekdays only, with seven stopping services northbound and two express trains taking twenty-five minutes non-stop, the second of them conveying through coaches from Hastings, Eastbourne, and Brighton to Sheffield. There was also a Northampton to Skegness service, which ran on Saturdays only. All these fast services crossed to the Midland at Market Harborough. The southbound pattern offered seven stopping services, one of them Mondays to Fridays only, one semi-fast train calling at Brixworth and Lamport and with conditional stops at Kelmarsh and Pitsford, an express from Leicester to Northampton conveying southbound through coaches for Brighton, Eastbourne, and Hastings, and a Skegness to Northampton train which ran on a limited number of summer Saturdays only. The non-stop time in this direction was also twenty-five minutes. The through coaches to and from the South Coast were worked south of Northampton by the splendidly-named 'Sunny South Express'. Such exotic services disappeared during the Second World War, in many cases never to be resurrected. In the equivalent month (July) of 1947, in the last year before nationalization, there were six passenger trains northbound and five southbound, weekdays only, and the service was basically all stations.

The *Sectional Appendix to the Working Timetable* for 1937 (which applied, with amendments, until 1960) shewed a line-speed of 50 m/h with lower limits of 35 round the curve at Little Bowden, 40 through Brixworth station, and 45 through Lamport station. Lie-by sidings (to use the LMS term) were provided at Kelmarsh and at Lamport, with capacities of 33 and 77 waggons respectively, and in both cases on the Up side of the line.

Intermediate traffic had never been heavy, and the stations were early candidates for closure. Spratton, which had never handled goods and which was so close to Brixworth, was closed entirely on 23 May 1949, and Pitsford soon followed, being closed to passenger traffic on 5 June 1950.[8] (Its counterpart on the Rugby line, Church Brampton, had been closed in 1931.) Brixworth, Lamport, Kelmarsh, and Clipston & Oxendon were closed to passenger traffic on 4 January 1960, when passenger services over the line officially ceased. Kelmarsh and Clipston & Oxendon were closed to goods traffic on the same date, and Brixworth and Lamport followed on 1 June 1964. Thus from the latter date the line was closed except as a through goods route and for traffic serving private sidings at Brixworth and Kelmarsh. It can thus be observed that full passenger closure and virtually complete goods closure had occurred on this line even before the infamous Beeching axe was swung. Other lines connecting with the Northampton & Harborough line were also closed, with the Blisworth to Northampton Castle section losing its passenger trains on 4 January 1960 (although it was used until 3 January 1966 for diversions during electrification, and the complete closure of the section as far as both Duston North Junction and Bridge Street junction did not take place until 6 January 1969). The service between Northampton Castle and Peterborough was

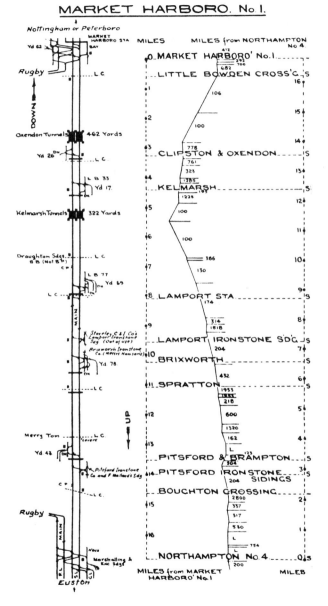

withdrawn on 4 May 1964, with complete closure of the line between Hardingstone junction and Wellingborough taking place on 1 August 1966.

Closures were similarly taking place at the northern end of the line. The Joint Line from Welham junction northwards had been closed to all passenger traffic except for a workmen's service on 7 December 1953, and the workmen's service from Market Harborough to East Norton ended on 20 May 1957. The line between Welham junction and Marefield North junction was closed completely on 4 November 1963. On 6 June 1966 the Rugby & Stamford line, together with its Seaton to Peterborough extension, was closed to all traffic as a result of the decision to concentrate all traffic between the West Midlands and East Anglia on the former Midland route through Nuneaton and Leicester rather than on the former LNW route through Rugby and Market Harborough. It is very interesting to note what was left: effectively it was the South Midland scheme of so long before, with a line from Leicester to Market Harborough splitting to run to Bedford on the one hand and Northampton and Roade on the other. But the standard of the route was very much lower than Francis Giles had envisaged in 1836, and lower than Robert Stephenson and Charles Liddell had planned in 1845. (As for the South Midland's proposed Huntingdon branch, even that had also been built in a simple form. This too was closed relatively early.) The major addition to the picture, by comparison with what had been envisaged previously, was the LNW Northampton to Rugby line, though it will be recalled that there had been pressure for some such route at a very early stage and that there were those 1846 powers for a connection to Weedon.

After the opening of the line to Rugby, Northampton was certainly given an improved service, even though the fastest trains to both Birmingham and the North continued to take the direct line through Weedon, as was to be expected. The Castle station became a place of an importance undreamed of when it was first opened as Northampton's second station (in both senses) in 1859. It will be remembered that the loop through Northampton was built as an alternative to the quadrupling of the main line, and as a result of this it has always been — logically enough — regarded as the continuation from Roade to Rugby of the slow lines, the pair of tracks normally used by goods trains. This partly accounts for the extensive marshalling facilities at Northampton, which in some ways corresponded in their position to those at Wellingborough on the Midland line and at Woodford Halse on the Great Central. These facilities were extended during the Second World War under the LMS programme of Wartime Works, when the junction at Kingsthorpe was also restored, its signalbox being Northampton No.5. It still remains true that drivers of trains can be directed through Northampton rather than over the main line through Weedon without any special advance warning.

There was one curiosity about the way in which working used to be carried out in the area. Running passenger trains over slow lines, especially fast passenger services, generally causes some interference with goods working, and in order to ease one aspect of this it became normal for Up passenger services calling at Northampton to return to the main line not over the direct route to Roade, but by way of the Duston junctions and Blisworth. This way they did not have to cross the Down slow line on the level and so interfere with other traffic. The alternative routes were thus used to provide a form of flyover, though one very unsuitable for fast passenger working on account of the sharp curves both at Duston and at Blisworth and the steep climb to the junction at the latter place.

Northampton Castle station was one of those chosen for complete rebuilding in the Euston-Manchester-Liverpool electrification programme, and quite a decent job was made of it. However, modernization did not extend to the layout, which was basically the old one perpetuated, as in so many other places on the LNW main line including Roade, where the junction had to be expensively replaced only a few years later by the modern installation at Hanslope. Even now, after many closures, the Northampton layout has not been improved: it has simply lost a number of connections and tracks that used to exist. Standard colour-light signalling was installed throughout the area, but control was not centralized. Thus trains approaching Northampton from the south leave the control of Rugby signalbox and come under the electro-mechanical installation at Northampton before returning to the supervision of Rugby further north. In one sense at least, Northampton still remains isolated from the main line! Nevertheless, within the town the Castle station survives as the solitary prosperous remnant of the Northampton & Harborough branch.

A study of the line to Market Harborough is not the place for an exhaustive examination of Northampton's train services, but the point must be made that neither the opening of the line to Market Harborough nor the completion of the loop to Rugby provided the sort of service to the North that the town had wished for. There can really be no doubt that Northampton has never recovered (in railway terms) from having been missed by the London & Birmingham main line. Although some attempt was made before the First World War to give a reasonable service to and from the main line, after that war and then after Grouping there was a failure to let Northampton share in the general improvement of the main-line service. There has been no major shift of policy over the last sixty years, and the service Northampton has today is very much inferior in terms of speed and comfort to that offered to Wellingborough and Kettering on the Midland main line in the same county, or to Peterborough (once administratively in Northamptonshire) on the Great Northern line. Wellingborough is almost exactly the same distance from London as Northampton, but it has a regular HST service, with the fastest trains taking only 45 minutes from London and even those serving all principal stations needing no more than 55 minutes.

The usefulness of the Harborough line as a through goods route continued, at least in part because the better connection between the Midland and the LNW systems, at Rugby, had so foolishly been completely closed on 1 January 1962. Its route was not protected and was later severed by building works, including the improvement of the A5 and the construction of the M1 motorway. In the 1960s the coal trains running between Toton and the Southern Region were diverted from Market Harborough by way of Northampton to Willesden instead of running via Cricklewood. But for such traffic as this the LNW branch was, of course, maintained to goods-line standards only, and it very soon became subject to a general speed-limit of 30 m/h.

A final period of glory began in January 1969, when the Midland line sleeper services between London and Scotland were diverted away from St Pancras in order to obviate the need to service sleeping cars at Cricklewood. A single train was provided from Euston at 9 p.m., running by way of Northampton and Market Harborough to Leicester, and then north by its normal route. The return working took the same route back to Euston, and provided the last regular day-time opportunity to travel over the Northampton & Harborough line. But this service finally petered out in arguments over closure procedures, and in the May 1973 timetable the sad remnant was a train at 1 a.m. (Mondays excepted) from Northampton to Leicester only. The line was also used by a certain amount of excursion traffic even after the withdrawal of scheduled services, and the timing of about an hour between Leicester and Northampton gave plenty of time to examine the scenery — or the works of the branch-line itself. The LNW platforms at Market Harborough were used from time to time for the Royal train, although the Down platform disappeared fairly early to make way for the commercial development of the site. The Up platform still remains, and presumably will do so until the completion of the modernization programme for Market Harborough.

There were other plans for the line. In the second Beeching Report there was a proposal to route main-line traffic between London and the East Midlands via Nuneaton to and from Euston.[9] But this idea does not appear to have been taken seriously for very long, and alternatives were considered. One of them involved the use of the Great Central line between Leicester and Rugby — a nice reversal of the 1891 Midland proposal — with new junction-curves at Whetstone and at Rugby. The junctions even received provisional names.[10] Another plan was to divert Midland main-line traffic at Market Harborough through Northampton to Euston — thus effectively over the South Midland Counties Railway! Electrification was considered between Northampton and Leicester. But this notion of turning the cheaply-built LNW branch of 1853-9 into a fast main line was really rather a joke, and early in 1967 it was reported that, in an East Midlands Traffic Study, British Railways had considered and rejected the idea of using the route through Northampton for express passenger traffic, although there were local rumours that electrification from Northampton to Toton for goods working had been contemplated and needed only government approval for the work to proceed, those being the distant and heady days when large-scale electrification was still expected.[11] It was not long after this that the plans for the grand rationalization of St Pancras and King's Cross were dropped, on various grounds, including terminal capacity, and the decision to keep and develop the Midland main line was taken.

Once such a decision had been taken, then it was inevitable that the future of the Northampton & Harborough line should be kept under close review, especially in the light of the pressures on British Railways to eliminate surplus track capacity. The amount of goods traffic moving over the line declined, and there was always the problem of the expense of the number of level crossings — an inheritance of the cheap construction. The 1980 *Sectional Appendix to the Working Timetable* shews that there were still no less than eight of them, four being operated from signalboxes which required manning if the line were to be used. Given this difficulty and the low speed restriction, the operating authorities often chose to run passenger traffic needing to get between the Midland and LNW lines via Nuneaton, with reversal at that point. And in the course of the West Hampstead re-signalling scheme, undertaken in connection with the London to Bedford suburban electrification programme, a new option was developed when the connection between the Midland and the LNW in Bedford was turned into a proper running junction. Thus there were two alternatives to the Northampton & Harborough line.

There was also another factor: development of the Midland main line includes plans for a major track re-alignment at Market Harborough to remove the badly-located 60 m/h speed restriction there. To have to include a junction in the re-alignment works would increase the cost considerably, and when it began to appear possible that the scheme might actually go ahead, either in connection with the Leicester re-signalling plans (which required only financial authorization in order to be allowed to proceed) or as a line-improvement scheme in its own right, it seemed likely that the often-rumoured closure of the line would not be long delayed. And so it proved, for closure took place on 15 August 1981.[12] Nothing much happened for many months, and it was not until the weekend of 12/13 June 1982 that the Up connection to the branch was removed together with its associated diamond crossing in the Down Midland line, plain line being substituted. The associated signalling was also taken away.[13] The Down connection remains for siding access, but that too will be cut when the re-alignment takes place, for the Midland running lines will have to be shifted right across to the LNW side of the formation to the north of Market Harborough station, and things will look very different indeed. However, it is interesting that at the time of writing (mid-1983) virtually no other demolition of the line has taken place, contrary to the practice in so many other cases of closure.

So the Northampton & Harborough line has come to the end of its life. Its final appearance seemed to indicate that it had been little more than a country branch line, and not perhaps a very interesting one at that. But this branch had its origins in the major controversies of the very early years of the railways, and it played a significant part in the railway politics of the complicated period of the 1870s, becoming the means by which the LNW gained access to important coal traffic from Nottinghamshire and South Yorkshire — traffic that the Company could surely not have foreseen as its own when it promoted the line in 1852/3. Twice there were possibilities that the line might become a part of a London trunk route — vaguely in 1890/91 and a little more strongly in the 1960s. So for a branch there is a history that is unusually rich and complex. Had developments been only a little different this line might not have been a branch at all, but rather a part of the modern Midland main line to London. But would matters have developed differently?

If the South Midland Counties line had been built in the 1830s then Midland traffic to London would have passed through Northampton. But there would still have been the pressures to build the Leicester & Hitchin line in one form or another in the 1840s, and there can be no doubt at all that the Great Northern main line would have been authorized. It seems reasonable to assume that the Midland's interests would still have meant that it would have felt obliged to be the company to build between Leicester and Hitchin. By the end of the 1840s, then, it may be assumed that the Midland would have had a main line to London by way of Northampton and the LNW, and also a long branch to join the Great Northern somewhere near Hitchin. Whether this situation would have come about as indicated above or by the building of the lines authorized to the Midland in 1847, the result would have been the same. The Midland would still have been dependent for its access to London on other companies, for a distance of some sixty miles over the LNW or some thirty miles over the Great Northern. There is no reason to suppose that the toll imposed on coal traffic over the Great Northern would have been lower, or that Parliament might have taken a different attitude to the 1852/3 amalgamation proposals between the Midland and the LNW. It seems only reasonable to suppose that the pressures which led the Midland to build its own line to London would still have been present and compelling.

For such a line the Midland would have been able to start at a point on the Hitchin line, or near Northampton. The shortest distance for new construction was from a point on the Hitchin line, and that could take the railway easily to the King's Cross/St Pancras area, where the company already had an establishment. The towns of Kettering, Wellingborough, and Bedford would be placed on the main line as useful sources of intermediate traffic, and Luton could be served. From Northampton southwards the territory cannot have looked nearly as potentially rewarding (as the Great Central later found), and there would have been a longer, and therefore more expensive, line to build. There was not a great deal of difference in the nature of the physical obstacles for either route. An argument that might have weighed if the 1836 line had been built rather than the 1847 line might have been the very good gradients that would have been available for coal traffic as far as Northampton, though this seems a little unlikely. In any case, the Midland may be assumed to have wished to stake a claim in East Leicestershire in the 1870s battles, and in doing so it was able very significantly to improve the gradients faced by its southbound coal traffic. It can reasonably be concluded that politics, working costs, and capital costs would have led to the development of the Midland main line, and the consequent relegation of the Northampton line to the status of a branch.

This branch would no doubt have survived until modern times, and if it had existed, then the possibility of re-routing Midland traffic to Euston and at the same time giving Northampton a better service — though at the expense of Kettering, Wellingborough, Bedford, and Luton —

might have been a very much more attractive one, for the route would have been suitable for very fast operation and so would have been a more reasonable alternative to the St Pancras main line. But in the end such speculation does not lead very far, as it takes account of only some might-have-beens in isolation from other equally possible might-have-beens (as, for example, the Oxford & Rugby line). And there are many more factors in any case that would have to be taken into account to draw sensible conclusions. What we are left to consider is what was actually built and used, and how it was built and used. The Northampton & Harborough line as finally constructed was built on the cheap. Nevertheless, it had a useful life, certainly under the ownership of its builders, the London & North Western, although there must be doubts as to whether it was ever really financially viable even for them. Under the LMS its position must be considered as more dubious, for it can certainly be argued that there was a strong case for some rationalization in the East Midlands after the former LNW lines and the former Midland lines had all come under the same management. Once the railways had been nationalized, the writing was clearly on the wall. Had the line been constructed to higher standards the 1960s might have provided a glorious future. Such was not to be.

REFERENCES

1 MT6 342/14
2 RAIL 410/64 (No. 129) and RAIL 410/113 Minute 48672
3 RAIL 418/4 Minute 359
4 RAIL 418/75 Minute 245
5 RAIL 418/93 Minutes 350, 374, 404, 429, 449, and 490
6 *Railway Gazette*, 18 April 1924, p. 587
7 RAIL 410/120 Minutes 4312, 4528, and 4594; RAIL 236/366
8 Closure dates from: C. R. CLINKER, *Clinker's Register of Closed Passenger Stations and Goods Depots in England, Scotland and Wales 1830-1977*, AvonAnglia Publications and Services, Bristol, 1978; Gerald DANIELS & Les DENCH, *Passengers No More*, 3rd edition, Ian Allan, 1980; N. J. HILL & A. O. McDOUGALL, *A Guide to Closed Railway Lines in Britain 1948-1975*, Branch Line Society, Huddersfield, 1977
9 *The Development of the Major Railway Trunk Routes*, British Railways Board, 1965
10 *British Railways National Route Code: Catalogue of Route Sections as at 1st January 1969*, British Railways Board 1969
11 *Railway Magazine*, November 1967, p. 108
12 Date from British Railways London Midland Region Operating Notices, e.g. *Periodical Operating Notice MED 49, 4 December 1982 - 4 February 1983*, p. 326
13 This date is from personal observation

Bibliography

PRIMARY MATERIALS

1. Public Record Office, Kew
   (All documents referred to which have citations beginning with 'RAIL', 'MT6', or 'MT7' are held in the Public Record Office.)

London and North Western Railway Company (RAIL 410)

Minutes of the Board of Directors
Minutes of the Committee of Special Affairs
Minutes of the Special Committee
Minutes of the Permanent Way, Works, and Estate Committee
Minutes of the Officers' Conference
Minutes of the General Traffic Committee
56, 62, 64, 68, 69 Reports to the Board
506   Rugby & Stamford &c. Committee
507   Branch Lines Committee
729   Reports to the Permanent Way Committee 1859
789   Northampton and Market Harborough branch, detailed land plan 1864-72
946   Kelmarsh, Clipston & Oxendon tunnels
1041 Contract plans for the Northampton stations
1042 Booking offices and buildings of the Northampton and Market Harborough branch
1195 Kelmarsh: plan of new sidings and platform
1214 Market Harborough joint station: general conditions
1239 Local Distance Table 1884, with 1887 Supplement
1254 General Manager's Circulars 1853-60
1291 Gradient table of all divisions
1541 Petition for station from Clipston
1564 Statement of costs of single mile of LNWR road
      Notice of public meeting in Northampton 1859
2032 Engineer's Cost of Works Ledger 1859-62
2036 Engineer's Cost of Works Ledger 1878-86
2048 L&NWR (Bletchley, Northampton & Rugby) Bill 1875 - papers
2054 L&NW and Midland Rlys (Market Harborough New Line and Works) Bill 1881: Parliamentary papers

Midland Railway Company (RAIL 491)

Minutes of the Board of Directors
Minutes of the Way & Works Committee
Minutes of the Traffic Committee
Minutes of the Parliamentary Committee
Minutes of the General Purposes Committee
299   Leicester & Hitchin Extension Committee
560   Plan of the Extension to Hitchin &c. 1846
672-7 Traffic and Expenses at Stations 1872-1922
709   Gradient tables, desk volume, 1902
830   Gradient profiles 1882
1145 Leicester to Hitchin extension, 1 to 31 miles, detailed plans and sections

Great Northern Railway Company (RAIL 236)

Minutes of the Board of Directors
Minutes of the Executive Committee
Minutes of the Traffic Committee
Reports to the Board: Arrangements with the Manchester, Sheffield, & Lincolnshire Railway 1890-94

RAIL 384/1   Minutes of the Board of Directors of the London & Birmingham Railway, Volume 1
RAIL 384/105   Minutes of the Northampton & Peterborough Committee
RAIL 406/14   Contract plans for Market Harborough 1883
RAIL 418/4   LMS Board Minutes I
RAIL 418/73   LMS Traffic Committee Minutes I
RAIL 418/93   LMS Works Committee Minutes I
RAIL 463   Minutes of the Board of Directors of the Manchester, Sheffield & Lincolnshire Railway
RAIL 637/1   Minutes of the Committee of the South Midland Railway
RAIL 1005/260   Chronology of the LNWR
RAIL 1005/289   Record of Opening and Closing Dates of the LNWR, continued by the LMS

RAIL 1007/205   Papers on the Northampton & Peterborough line
RAIL 1008/111   Catalogue of letters in the Euston collection
RAIL 1008/112   Reports from G. R. Stephenson on the state of works on the Northampton and Market Harborough line
RAIL 1015/2   Historical Records, Papers, &c.
RAIL 1020/2   Handbills and Notices
RAIL 1066/1095 Proceedings of the Parliamentary Committees on the Great Northern and Midland & Manchester, Sheffield & Lincolnshire Railways' Bills 1873
RAIL 1066/1099 Proceedings of the Parliamentary Committees on the Great Northern and London & North Western Railways' Bill 1874
RAIL 1066/1541 Proceedings of the Parliamentary Committees on the London & Birmingham Railway Bill 1832
RAIL 1075/432   Prospectus and Map of the South Midland Counties Railway 1836
RAIL 1110/175   Great Northern and London & North Western Joint Line, Accounts
RAIL 1110/279   LNWR Reports and Accounts
RAIL 1110/329   Midland Railway Reports and Accounts
RAIL 1124/11   Select Committee on Subscription Lists
RAIL 1153/13   Leicester & Bedford Railway circulars
RAIL 1160/85   South Midland Railway, Indenture

Public and Working Timetables of the Great Northern Railway for various years (RAIL 935), Working Timetables of the London & North Western Railway for various years (RAIL 946), and Working Timetable of the London, Midland, & Scottish Railway (Midland Section: Passenger) 1924 (RAIL 957/4)

Board of Trade, Railway Department

MT6   17/28   LNWR Northampton & Market Harborough branch 1858
MT6   17/48   -ditto-   1858
MT6   17/64   -ditto-   1858
MT6   17/66   LNWR level crossing
MT6   24/14   LNWR Castle station to Nene viaduct 1861
MT6   25/41   LNWR Northampton to Market Harborough branch 1861
MT6   157/6   Railways: opening postponements; Law Officers' opinion 1876

MT6   181/13   LNWR Market Harborough 1876-1877
MT6   209/16b LNWR Kingsthorpe 1878
MT6   246/5   LNWR Lamport to Market Harborough 1879-1880
MT6   255/7   LNWR Bletchley, Northampton & Rugby branch 1880
MT6   260/5   LNWR Northampton, Bridge Street Jcn 1880
MT6   281/7   LNWR Northampton to Market Harborough; Rugby to Stamford; Bletchley to Roade; signalling 1878-1881
MT6   307/7   LNWR Kingsthorpe Junction 1882
MT6   310/10   LNWR Bletchley to Northampton & Rugby 1881-1882
MT6   342/14   LNWR Brixworth station 1883
MT6   353/6   LNWR Market Harborough 1882-1885
MT6   381/12   MR Market Harborough 1885
MT6   386/9   LNWR Northampton station 1885
MT6   387/8   LNWR Rugby 1882-1885
MT6   389/5   MR Market Harborough 1885
MT6   416/1   LNWR Market Harborough 1883-1886

MT7   23   Index 1856
MT7   24   Register 1856
MT7   27   Index 1858
MT7   28   Register 1858
MT7   29   Index 1859
MT7   30   Register 1859
MT7   31   Index 1860
MT7   32   Register 1860
MT7   33   Index 1861
MT7   34   Register 1861
MT7   35   Index 1862
MT7   37   Index 1863
MT7   92   Index 1882
MT7   97   Index 1883

2. Leicestershire County Record Office (=LRO)
    Deposited Railway Plans
    QS 73/ 60   Leicester & Bedford Railway 1845
    QS 73/102   South Midland or Leicester, Northampton, Bedford, and Huntingdon Railways 1845
    QS 73/108   Midland Railway Extensions 1846 (Leicester to Hitchin and to Northampton & Huntingdon)
    QS 73/114   Midland Railway Extension from Leicester to Hitchin 1852
    QS 73/135   Midland Railway (Additional Powers) 1861
    QS 73/225   Midland Railway (New Works &c.) 1876

QS 73/231 London & North Western Rly (New Lines) 1876

QS 73/249 London & North Western and Midland Railways (Market Harborough New Line and Works) 1880

(N.B. The last four items all refer to Market Harborough.)

3. Northamptonshire County Record Office (=NRO)
QS Deposited Plans (London & North Western Railway)

66 Northampton to Market Harborough 1852

70 Additional lands St Peter's Northampton 1857

73 Deviation at Lamport 1858

149 Bletchley, Northampton and Rugby 1874

163 Long Buckby footpath and Northampton (Castle) Station 1877

L(C) 1309-10, 1359 Letters from Joseph Tatham to Herbert Langham

YZ 6221-31 Correspondence about Lord Bateman's land

BHB 50 Correspondence about Boughton Level Crossing

MAPS 3165 Northampton to Rugby line plan 1874

MAPS 3743-4 Progress plans for the Kelmarsh and Oxendon new tunnels

MAPS 3745 Northampton to Kingsthorpe Widening plan 1881

4. Northampton Central Library
Files (microfilm) of the *Northampton Mercury* and the *Northampton Herald*

5. British Library, London

(a) Acts of Parliament

(1) An Act for making a Railway, with Branches, commencing at the London and Birmingham Railway in the Parish of Rugby in the County of Warwick, to communicate with the Towns of Leicester, Nottingham, and Derby, to be called, 'The Midland Counties Railway.'   6 William IV cap. lxxviii

(2) An Act for making a Branch Railway from the London and Birmingham Railway to Northampton and Peterborough   6 & 7 Victoria cap. lxiv

(3) The Rugby and Stamford Railway Act 1846
                9 Victoria cap. lxvii

(4) The London and Birmingham Railway, Weedon and Northampton Branch, Act 1846
                9 & 10 Victoria cap. cccix

(5) The Midland Railways, Extension to Hitchin, Northampton, and Huntingdon, Act 1847
                10 & 11 Victoria cap. cxxxv

(6) The Midland Railway (Leicester and Hitchin) Act 1853   16 & 17 Victoria cap. cviii

(7) The London and North Western Railway (Northampton and Market Harborough &c. Branches) Act 1853   16 & 17 Victoria cap. clx

(8) The London and North Western Railway (Additional Works) Act 1858 21 & 22 Victoria cap. cxxxi

(9) The London and North Western Railway (New Works) Act 1859   22 & 23 Victoria cap. cxiii

(10) The Great Northern and London and North-western Railway Companies (Joint Powers and New Lines) Act 1874   37 & 38 Victoria cap. clvii

(11) The London and North-western Railway (England and Ireland) Act 1874   37 & 38 Victoria cap. clix

(12) The London and North-western Railway (Bletchley, Northampton, and Rugby) Act 1875
                38 & 39 Victoria cap. cii

(13) The London and North-western Railway (Additional Powers) Act 1878 41 & 42 Victoria cap. clxxxi

(14) The London and North-western and Midland Railway Companies (Market Harborough Line) Act 1881   44 Victoria cap. xlvii

(15) The London and North-western Railway (New Railways) Act 1881   44 & 45 Victoria cap. cxli

Public Acts: The Railway Regulation Act 1842
        The Railway Clauses Act 1863

(b) Maps

The relevant sheets of the various editions of the 25″ and 6″ plans of the Ordnance Survey

BOOKS & ARTICLES

E. G. Barnes, *The Rise of the Midland Railway 1844-1874*, George Allen & Unwin, 1966

E. G. Barnes, *The Midland Main Line 1875-1922*, George Allen & Unwin, 1969

Bradshaw's *Railway Guides*, various dates

Bradshaw's *Railway Shareholders' Guide and Manual*, various dates

British Railways Board, *British Railways National Route Code: Catalogue of Route Sections as at 1st January 1969*, British Railways Board, 1969

British Railways Board, *The Development of the Major Railway Trunk Routes*, British Railways Board, 1965

C. R. Clinker, *Clinker's Register of Closed Passenger Stations and Goods Depots in England, Scotland and Wales 1830-1977*, AvonAnglia Publications and Services, Bristol, 1978

C. R. Clinker, *The Railways of Northamptonshire (including the Soke of Peterborough) 1800-1960*, published by the author, Rugby, 1960

Gerald Daniels & Les Dench, *Passengers No More*, 3rd edition, Ian Allan, 1980

George Dow, *Great Central*, 3 volumes, Locomotive Publishing Company, 1959-65

George Findlay, *The Working and Management of an English Railway*, 6th edition, Whittaker & Company, 1899

Richard D. Foster, *A Pictorial Record of L.N.W.R. Signalling*, Oxford Railway Publishing Company, Poole, 1982

T. R. Gourvish, *Mark Huish and the London & North Western Railway: a study of management*, Leicester University Press, 1972

T. R. Gourvish, *Railways and the British Economy 1830-1914*, Macmillan Press, 1980

Charles H. Grinling, *The History of the Great Northern Railway*, with additional chapters by H. V. Borley and C. Hamilton Ellis, George Allen & Unwin, 1966

Victor A. Hatley, 'Northampton Hoodwinked? How a Main Line of Railway Missed the Town a Second Time', *Journal of Transport History*, VII (3), 1966, pp. 160-72

Victor A. Hatley, 'Northampton Re-vindicated: More Light on Why the Main Line Missed the Town', *Northamptonshire Past and Present* II (6), 1959, pp. 305-9

N. J. Hill & A. O. McDougall, *A Guide to Closed Railway Lines in Britain 1948-1975*, Branch Line Society, Huddersfield, 1977

A Landed Proprietor, *Address to the Land Owners, Land Occupiers, and Others who have signed a Petition to the House of Commons against the Proposed Line of Railroad from Leicester through Harborough to Northampton and Blisworth*, Thomas Abbot, Market Harborough, 1836

Robin Leleux, *A Regional History of the Railways of Great Britain, Volume 9, The East Midlands*, David & Charles, Newton Abbot, 1976

Henry Grote Lewin, *The Railway Mania and its Aftermath*, Railway Gazette, 1936

G. C. Lewthwaite, *Branch Line Index*, 2nd edition, Branch Line Society, Timperley, 1971

H. I. Longden, *Northamptonshire and Rutland Clergy*, 15 volumes in 5 with another volume as Supplement by other authors, Archer & Goodman, Northampton, 1938-42 & 1952

John Marshall, *A Biographical Dictionary of Railway Engineers*, David & Charles, Newton Abbot, 1978

Philip R. Martin, 'Rothwell; the Railway Station that never was', *Northamptonshire Past and Present* VI (3), 1980, pp. 161-4

G. P. Neele, *Railway Reminiscences*, McCorquodale & Co., 1904

Andrew C. O'Dell & Peter S. Richards, *Railways and Geography*, 2nd edition, Hutchinson, 1971

Henry Parris, *Government and the Railways in Nineteenth-Century Britain*, Routledge & Kegan Paul, 1965

R. M. Serjeantson, *The Castle of Northampton*, Joseph Tebbutt, Northampton, 1908

J. Simmons, 'Communication and Transport' in N. Pye (Ed), *Leicester and its Region*, Leicester University Press, 1972, pp. 311-24

J. Simmons, *The Railway in England and Wales 1830-1914, Volume 1, The System and its Working*, Leicester U.P., 1978

J. Simmons, 'Railways', in W. G. Hoskins & R. A. McKinley (eds), *A History of the County of Leicester, Volume III*, Oxford University Press for the Institute of Historical Research 1955

Wilfred L. Steel, *The History of the London & North Western Railway*, The Railway and Travel Monthly, 1914

David Stevenson, *Fifty Years on the London & North Western Railway*, McCorquodale & Co., 1891

Clement E. Stretton, *The History of the Midland Railway*, Methuen, 1901

E. S. Tonks, *The Ironstone Railways and Tramways of the Midlands*, Locomotive Publishing Company, 1961

o. V., *Das Deutsche Eisenbahnwesen der Gegenwart*, 2 volumes, Reimar Hobbing, Berlin, 1911

Joan Wake, *Northampton Vindicated or Why the Main Line Missed the Town*, published by the author, Northampton, 1935

Francis Whishaw, *Analysis of Railways*, John Weale, 1837

Francis Whishaw, *The Railways of Great Britain and Ireland*, 2nd edition, John Weale, 1842

Frederick S. Williams, *The Midland Railway: its Rise and Progress*, 3rd edition, Bemrose & Company, 1877

Frederick S. Williams, *Our Iron Roads*, 3rd edition, Bemrose & Sons, 1883

John Wrottesley, *The Great Northern Railway*, 3 volumes, Batsford, 1979-81

Appendix A

Table of Distances

The following table, which gives distances from the zero-point of the Northampton & Harborough line at Duston West Junction, is a conflation of figures from a number of different sources.

			0m	0000yds
Duston West junction				
Duston North junction			0	638
Northampton No. 1			0	1224
Roade line junction			0	1310
Northampton Castle station			0	1537
Northampton No. 2			0	1686
Northampton No. 3			1	345
Northampton No. 4			1	1243
Northampton No. 5			2	286
Boughton Crossing			3	1650
Pitsford and Brampton		app.	4	1540
Merry Tom Crossing		app.	5	1210
Spratton		app.	7	660
Spratton Crossing			7	830
Brixworth		app.	8	176
Hanging Houghton Crossing		app.	9	968
Isham Crossing		app.	10	264
Lamport Crossing			10	682
Lamport			10	1100
Draughton Crossing			11	1298
Green Lane Crossing		app.	12	440
Kelmarsh tunnel	from		13	47
	to		13	578
Kelmarsh			14	0000
Clipston and Oxendon		app.	15	220
Oxendon tunnel	from		15	1155
	to		15	1617
Little Bowden Crossing			17	1650
Market Harborough No. 1			18	836
Market Harborough station			18	1166
Market Harborough No. 2			18	1298
Market Harborough No. 3			18	1694
Bridge Street junction			0	0000
Duston North junction			0	395
Blisworth junction			0	0000
Duston West junction			3	1694
Bridge Street junction			4	638
Bridge Street station, Northampton			4	1144

The end of the line at closure was at 19 miles 8 chains from the zero-point, which was equal to 83 miles 30 chains from London St Pancras on the Midland main line at the point of junction in Market Harborough.

Appendix B

The extracts on the following four pages shew the passenger service over the Northampton & Harborough line at the time of its opening in 1859, in June 1861, when a regular pattern of service had had a chance to develop, and in August 1911 — a summer season shortly before the great changes brought about by the First World War and its aftermath.

The first extract is from the *Northampton Mercury* for 26 February 1859, and shews the LNW advertisement with its small and attractive woodcut illustration surrounded by a miscellany of other advertising matter in a provincial newspaper. The second and third extracts are from the appropriate editions of *Bradshaw's Guide*, the third shewing services together with those for the GN & LNW Joint Line.

The final extract, eleven pages in length, is of a different nature. It is taken from the Working Timetable of the Nottingham, Northampton and Peterboro' Division of the London & North Western Railway *(Time Tables for Enginemen, Guards, Breaksmen and Others)* issued for July 1883. From the material reproduced it is possible to see exactly what traffic was flowing through Northampton and Market Harborough in all directions at a period when the new lines and facilities in Northampton had been opened but before the Midland and LNW traffic at Market Harborough had been segregated by the building of the new joint station. All trains are clearly identified. The meaning of the symbols is as follows:

> Trains running on the Fast lines between Northampton and Kingsthorpe junction are indicated in normal type, with those using the Slow lines (the Northampton & Harborough line) being shewn in italic type.

C = Conditional train
M = Train does not run on Mondays
x = Train stop only if required to do so
S = Train stops to set down if notice is given to the Guard at the previous stopping station, or to pick up if signalled to do so at the station in question
* = Train stops for locomotive purposes, examination, etc., or to shunt for other trains to pass, NOT to attach or detach Waggons

FOR RHEUMATISM, FEVERS, COUGHS, COLDS, &c.

IN all the various forms of these complaints, from which numbers suffer so severely, particularly during the Winter Months, a more salutary Remedy cannot be resorted to, or one that has effected more extraordinary Cures, than the Genuine *Bateman's Pectoral Drops*, which may be purchased at the Original Warehouse, No. 10, Bow Church Yard, Cheapside, and at most respectable Medicine Venders either in Town or County. Like many other valuable Medicines, however, it is very much counterfeited, which renders it the more necessary for Purchasers to be particular in inquiring for "DICEY'S *Bateman's Drops*," which have the words "DICEY & Co." in the Stamp, and are the only genuine sort. In bottles, price 1s. 1½d. and 2s. 9d. each.

LONDON AND NORTH-WESTERN RAILWAY.

Direct Route to Market Harborough and Stamford.

THE NORTHAMPTON AND MARKET HARBO-ROUGH LINE is NOW OPEN for Passenger Traffic, and TRAINS will RUN DAILY (Sundays excepted,) as under, for the Month of FEBRUARY :—

UP TRAINS.	1,2,3. Class	1 & 2 Class	DOWN TRAINS.	1,2,3. Class	1 & 2 Class
	a.m.	p.m.		a.m.	p.m.
LEAVE			LEAVE		
Stamford........	8.45	2.10	London	9.15	2.45
ARRIVE AT			Blisworth ...	11. 5	4.25
Market Harboro'	9.40	3. 5	ARRIVE AT		
Lamport........	10. 2	3.27	Northampton....	11.15	4.35
Northampton....	10.30	3.55	Lamport.......	11.45	5. 5
Blisworth	10 40	4. 5	Market Harboro'	12. 5	5.25
London	2. 0	6.15	Stamford.......	1. 0	6.20
		Aft.	Aft.	Aft.	Aft.

By order,
W. CAUKWELL, General Manager.
Euston Station, 18 Feb., 1859.

HENRI'S PATENT HORSE AND CATTLE FEED.

HENRI'S Patent Horse and Cattle Feed Company having secured the above Patents, and having taken and entered upon the Premises where the above Meals have been previously manufactured, beg to call the attention of Agriculturists to the same, assuring them that the article shall be in every respect equal to the quality which obtained for it its celebrity when first introduced three years ago.
Hull, December, 1858.

For Testimonials, price, &c., apply to HENRI'S PATENT CATTLE FEED COMPANY, STEAM MILLS, HULL, or to our AGENTS, as under :—
NORTHAMPTON and DISTRICT—Mr. EDWARD TRESHAM.
WELLINGBOROUGH and DISTRICT—Mr. JOHN SMITH. Coal Wharf.
HARTWELL and DISTRICT—Mr. GEORGE BLISS.
ROTHWELL and DISTRICT—Mr. GUE.
OUNDLE and DISTRICT—Mr. GRAVELY.

HELLIDON, near Daventry.

THOMAS EALES

WILL SELL BY AUCTION,

On FRIDAY, MARCH 4TH, 1859, subject to the usual credit, 14 OAK, 6 ASH, and 10 ELM TIMBER TREES, most of which are of long lengths and of good size, now blazed and

SALE OF 614 PURE-BRED SHROPSHIRE SHEEP,

At MERIDEN.

Mr. HENRY BROWN

WILL SELL BY AUCTION,

On WEDNESDAY, the 2ND of MARCH, 1859, at the HEATH FARM, MERIDEN ;

THE FLOCK of 614 pure-bred Shrop-shire SHEEP, consisting of—
230 EWES and THEAVES, in lamb or with lambs,
180 EWE TEGS,
140 WETHER DITTO,
36 RAM TEGS,
13 Shearhog and older RAMS,
15 Fat two-shear WETHERS,
The property of the Right Hon. the Earl of AYLESFORD.
Luncheon on the Table at half-past Ten, and the Sale to commence at half-past Twelve o'clock.
The Place of Sale is within 3 Miles of the Hampton Station, on the London and North Western Railway ; 7 Miles from Coventry ; and 10 Miles from Birmingham.
Catalogues are ready, and may be had at the office of this Paper ; of Mr. Sharp, Farm Bailiff, upon the Farm, and of the Auctioneer, 11, Corn Exchange Buildings, Hertford Street, Coventry, who will forward the same by post on application.

MR. WILLIAM WATTS, deceased.

ALL Persons having Claims upon the ESTATE of WILLIAM WATTS, late of SCALDWELL, in the County of Northampton, Farmer, are requested, forthwith, to send the particulars to Mr. Thomas Underwood, of Sywell Hall, in the said County, Mr. James Knight Deacon, of 42, Alfred-street, Islington, London, or Mr. Joseph Ireland, of Brixworth, in the said County, the Executors. And all persons indebted the said Estate are requested to pay such Debts to the said Joseph Ireland forthwith.
Dated 16th February, 1859.

A. & H. MARKHAM, ⎱ Solicitors to the
R. C. ANDREW, ⎰ Executors.

Mr. THOMAS COOPER, deceased.

NOTICE TO DEBTORS AND CREDITORS.

ALL Persons who have any Claims or Demands upon the Estate of Mr. THOMAS COOPER, late of PETSOE, in the county of Buckingham, Farmer, deceased, are requested to send particulars thereof to me, the under-signed.
And all persons who stood Indebted to the said Thomas Cooper at the time of his decease, are desired to pay the amount of their respective debts to Mr. Cooper Cardwell, of Northampton, Lace Merchant, one of the Executors of the deceased.
By order of the Executors,
WILLIAM TOMALIN, Jun., their Solicitor.
Market-square, Northampton, Feb. 24, 1859.

WHEREAS a Petition of JOHN MOORE, of ROWELL, in the county of Northampton, Black-smith and Farmer, an INSOLVENT DEBTOR, having been filed in the County Court of Northamptonshire, holden at Kettering, in the said county, and an Interim Order for Protection from Process having been given to the said John Moore, under the provisions of the Statutes in that case made and provided, the said John Moore is hereby required to appear in the said Court to be holden at the ROYAL HOTEL, KETTERING aforesaid, before the Judge of the said Court, on the NINETEENTH day of MARCH next, at Eleven o'clock in the Forenoon precisely, for his First Examination touching his debts, estate, and effects, and to be further dealt with according to the provisions of the said Statutes. And Notice is hereby given, That the choice of Assignees is to take place at the time so appointed. All persons indebted to the said John Moore, or who have any of his effects, are not to pay or deliver the same, but

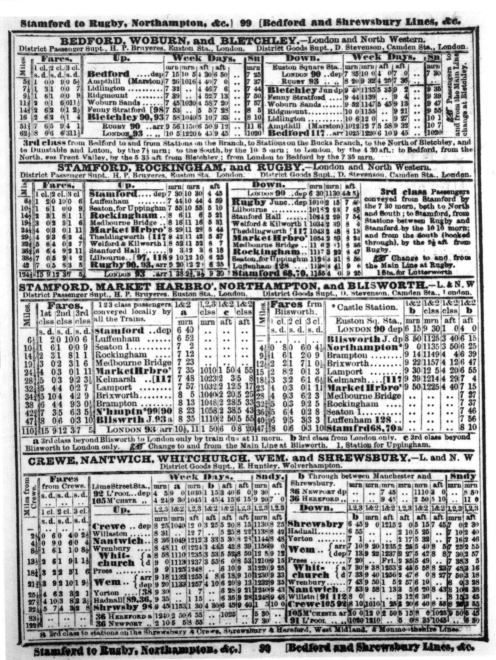

BEDFORD, WOBURN, and BLETCHLEY.—London and North Western.
District Passenger Supt., H. P. Bruyeres, Euston Sta., London.   District Goods Supt., D. Stevenson, Camden Sta., London.

3rd class from Bedford to and from Stations on the Branch, to Stations on the Bucks Branch, to the North of Bletchley, and to Dunstable and Luton, by the 7¼ mrn; to the South, by the 10 5 mrn; to London, by the 4 30 aft.; to Bedford, from the North, via Trent Valley, by the 5 35 aft from Bletchley; from London to Bedford by the 7 35 mrn.

STAMFORD, ROCKINGHAM, and RUGBY.—London and North Western.
District Passenger Supt., H. P. Bruyeres, Euston Sta., London.   District Goods Supt., D. Stevenson, Camden Sta., London.

STAMFORD, MARKET HARBRO', NORTHAMPTON, and BLISWORTH.—L. & N. W
District Passenger Supt., H. P. Bruyeres, Euston Sta., London.   District Goods Supt., D. Stevenson, Camden Sta., London.

a 3rd class beyond Blisworth to London only by train due at 11 morn.   b 3rd class from London only.   c 3rd class beyond Blisworth to London only.   Change to and from the Main Line at Blisworth.   1, Station for Uppingham.

CREWE, NANTWICH, WHITCHURCH, WEM, and SHREWSBURY.—L. and N. W
District Goods Supt., E. Huntley, Wolverhampton.

a 3rd class to stations on the Shrewsbury & Crewe, Shrewsbury & Hereford, West Midland, & Monmouthshire Lines.

Bradshaw's Guide, June 1861 (Leicester University Library)

Newark, Grantham, Nottingham, **380** Leicester, Market Harboro', & Northampton.

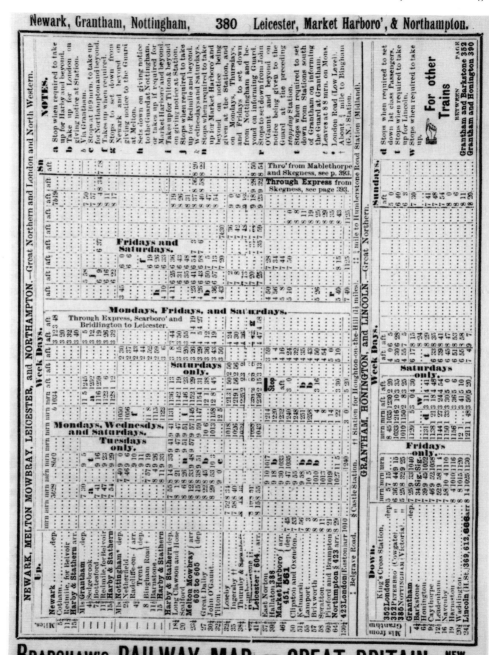

NEWARK, MELTON MOWBRAY, LEICESTER, and NORTHAMPTON.—Great Northern and London and North Western.

GRANTHAM, HONINGTON, and LINCOLN.—Great Northern.

BRADSHAW'S RAILWAY MAP OF GREAT BRITAIN. NEW EDITION.

Bradshaw's Guide, August 1911 (Leicester University Library)

Northampton and Newark.]　381　[G. N. and L. & N. W.

NORTHAMPTON, LEICESTER, MELTON MOWBRAY, and NEWARK.—Great Northern and London and North Western.

NOTES.

a　Wednesdays and Saturdays. Arrives at 7.59 aft. on Sats. Takes up when required. Via Grantham.
b　By slip carriage.
c　Stops to set down 1st class Passengers from London at Northampton.
d　Stops to set down on giving notice to the Guard at North-ampton.
e　Stops to set down from Lon-don (Euston) on informing the Guard at the preceding *stopping* Station.
f　Sets down from Melton Mowbray and beyond.
g　Stops to set down from Northampton and beyond.
h　Stops to set down from the Joint Line and beyond on informing the Guard at Radcliffe-on-Trent.
i　Tues., Fris., and Sats.
j　Stops on Saturdays at 12 49 aft. to take up.
k　Sets down if required.
l　Tuesdays and Saturdays.
o　Takes up when required for Newark and beyond.
v　Sets down on informing Guard at preceding *stopping* station.

☞ **For other Trains**
BETWEEN　PAGE
Leicester and Tilton..　388
Radcliffe-on-Trent and Nottingham..　382
Bottesford & Grantham..　385

Other Trains

☞　Stop to take up for London.
§§　London Road (Low Level Station).

BETWEEN　PAGE
Barkstone & Grantham..　359
Honington & Grantham..　392

Down. Week Days.

* London Rd. (L.L.) Bingham (G.N.) Station.
† About ¾ mile to Belgrave Road.

Buffet Car, Bottesford to Skegness. Ar. Skegness 7 30 aft.

Thro' to Skegness and Mablethorpe, see p. 390.

Through Train to Bridlington & Scarboro'.

Miles — Stations (Down):
Euston Station....dep.
41½ London....dep.
Northampton §....dep.
Pitsford and Brampton.
6½ Spratton
7½ Brixworth
9¼ Lamport
11½ Kelmarsh
14¼ Clipston and Oxendon
Market Harboro' { arr. dep.
　451, 581
18 Hallaton 388
27 East Norton
Mls Leicester §....dep.
1¾ Humberstone †
3½ Thurnby & Scraptoft
6¼ Ingersby ††
9½ Lowesby
31 Tilton 380
37 John O'Gaunt
37½ Great Dalby
41½ Melton Mowbray { arr. dep.
　603 to 605
44 Scalford
46½ Long Clawson and Hose
49 Harby & Stathern { arr. dep.
Harby & Stathern....dep.
52¾ Bingham Road †
56 Radcliffe-on-Trent 382, 385 { arr. dep.
59¾ Netherfield 389
61½ Nottingham *....arr.
Harby & Stathern....dep.
Redmile, for Belvoir.
Bottesford.
Sedgebrook 359, 380
60 Grantham 352....arr.
Newark §§ 352, 612....arr.
64¾ § Castle Station.

Up. Week Days.

LINCOLN, HONINGTON, and GRANTHAM.—Great Northern.

Mls Stations (Up):
High Street Station....dep.
Lincoln
4½ Waddington
5½ Harmston
8 Navenby
12¼ Leadenham
13 Caythorpe
18¾ Honington 390
20½ Barkstone
24¾ Grantham 359, 382
48 382 Nottingham (Victoria)....arr.
53¾ 359 Peterboro' (Cowgate)....arr.
130 359 London (King's Cross)....arr.

‡ Station for Houghton-on-the-Hill 1½ miles.　§ About 1 mile to Midland Station.
‖ 1 mile to Humberstone Road Station, Midland.　† Station for Houghton-on-the-Hill.

Revised and corrected to date. Divided in Lettered Squares, with marginal List of Stations. Price 1/9, post free. Printed on Linen, Varnished, and with Metal Fittings and Hanger, 3/-

4

Trains between Northampton (Castle Jun.) and Kingsthorpe Jun.

DOWN TRAINS.

Description.	Northampton (Castle) arr. a.m.	dep. a.m.	pass a.m.	Kingsthorpe Junction. pass a.m.	Remarks.
Express Goods C	...	...	12 12	12 17	9.25 p.m. Camden to Rugby.
,, ,, M	...	...	12 28	12 33	9.10 p.m. Broad Street to B'ham.
Goods ... M	12 30	...	...	...	12.15 a.m. ex Blisworth.
Express Goods M	12 35	12 45	...	12 50	9.40 p.m. Camden to Doncaster.
Empties (Mondays only) ...	...	1 15	...	1 20	For Doncaster.
Express Pass. ...	1 31	1 33	...	1 37	12.0 night Euston to Rugby.
Express Goods M	2 8	2 13	...	2 18	11.10 p.m. Camden to Nott'ngham
Express Goods M	...	..	2 27	2 32	For Rugby.
Goods&Empties M	2 50	3 20	...	3 25	2.45 a.m. Bridge Street to Rugby
Empties ... M	...	...	3 32	3 37	12.25 a.m. Willesden to Rugby.
,, ... M C	...	3 30	...	3 35	For Doncaster.
Goods&Empties M	3 40	4 0	...	4 5	12.35 a.m. Willesden to Rugby.
Empties ... M	4 0	4 10	...	4 15	12.55 a.m. Willesden to Colwick.
,, ... C	...	...	4 25	4 30	1.15 a.m. Willesden to Rugby.
,, ... M	...	...	4 40	4 45	1.30 a.m. Willesden to Stafford.
,, ... M	4 15	4 45	...	4 50	1.0 a.m. Camden to Colwick.
Empties ... M	...	5 45	...	5 50	For Doncaster (1.15 a.m. on Mondays,)
Express Pass. ... C	6 37	6 39	...	6 43	5.15 a.m. Euston to Rugby.
Empties ... C	...	7 0	...	7 5	For Doncaster.
Pass.	...	7 30	...	7 34	,, Nottingham.
Empties M C	...	7 40	...	7 45	,, Colwick.
Stock Train ... C	...	...	8 0	8 5	7.30 a.m. Wolverton to Crewe.
Pass.	...	8 15	...	8 19	For Rugby.
Empties ... M	8 15	8 20	...	8 25	4.45 a.m. Willesden to Rugby.
,, ... C	8 25	8 35	...	8 40	5.0 a.m. Willesden to Colwick.
,, ... C	8 50	9 20	...	9 25	5.30 a.m. Willesden to Doncaster
Express Pass. ...	9 4	9 6	...	9 10	7.30 a.m. Euston to Rugby.
Pass.	9 14	9 15	...	9 19	For Nottingham.
Empties M C	...	9 30	...	9 55	,, Colwick.
,, ...	...	...	9 40	9 45	6.0 a.m. Willesden to Wigan.
,, (Tuesdays only.) ...	...	9 45	...	9 50	For Colwick.
Ironstone ... C	9 50	10 5	...	10 10	,, Great Bowden (9.45 a.m. from Bridge Street)
Express Pass. ...	10 40	10 42	...	10 46	9.0 a.m. Euston to Rugby.
Goods	10 45	11 0	...	11 5	For Great Bowden Sidings. (10.0 a.m. from Bridge Street.)
Express Pass. ...	...	10 48	...	10 52	For Nottingham.
,, ,, ...	10 54	10 57	...	11 1	9.30 a.m. Euston to Birmingham
Empties ... C	...	11 35	...	11 40	For Colwick.
Express Pass. ...	11 55	11 57	...	12 1	9.15 a.m. Euston to Rugby.
Empties	12 25	12 35	...	12 40	9.30 a.m. Willesden to Rugby.
Express Pass. ...	12 54	12 57	...	1 1	11.30 a.m. Euston to Birmingham
G. N. Pass. ...	...	1 0	...	1 4	For Notts.
Empties ... C	12 40	1 5	...	1 10	11.45 a.m. Bletchley to Colwick.
Ironstone	1 5	1 15	...	1 20	For Rugby. (6.0 a.m. ex Peterboro'.)
Empties ... C	1 25	1 35	...	1 40	10.0 a.m. Willesden to Colwick.
Express Pass. ...	1 51	1 54	...	1 58	12.15 p.m. Euston to Rugby.
Pass.	...	2 25	...	2 29	For Rugby.
,, ...	...	2 30	...	2 34	,, Nottingham.
Goods	2 15	2 35	...	2 40	,, Rugby (2.0 p.m. from Bridge St.)
Empties	...	2 40	...	2 45	For Retford.
,, ... C	2 50	3 0	...	3 5	11.30 a.m. Willesden to Doncaster
,, ... C	...	...	3 2	3 7	11.40 a.m. Willesden to Rugby.
Ironstone	3 40	...	...	...	From Duston Sidings (Gas Siding arr. 3.25 dep.3.35)
,, ... C	...	3 55	...	4 0	For Doncaster.
Express Pass. ...	3 54	3 57	...	4 1	2.30 p.m. Euston to Birmingham
,, ,, ...	...	4 0	...	4 4	For Nottingham.

LNWR Working Timetable, July 1883 (Public Record Office. By permission of British Rail)

5

Trains between Northampton (Castle Jun.) and Kingsthorpe Jun,

DOWN TRAINS—*Continued.*

Description.	Northampton (Castle). arr. p.m.	dep. p.m.	pass p.m.	Kingsthorpe Junction. pass p.m	Remarks.
Goods & Empties...	4 35	5 15	...	5 20	2.25 p.m. Tring to Rugby.
Pass.	4 45	4 47	...	4 51	1.55 ,, Euston ,,
,, ...	...	4 50	...	4 54	For Nottingham.
Empties ... **C**	...	5 10	...	5 15	,, Colwick.
Pass.	5 20	6 0	...	6 4	3.10 p.m. Euston to Rugby.
Express Pass. ...	5 54	5 57	...	6 1	4.30 ,, ,, Birmingham.
Express Pass ...	...	6 0	...	6 4	For Nottingham.
Empties ...	6 10	6 15	...	6 20	5.5 p.m. Bletchley to Colwick.
,, ...	6 30	6 40	...	6 45	3.0 ,, Willesden to ,,
Express Pass. ...	6 50	6 53	...	6 57	5.15 ,, Euston to Rugby.
Empty Waggons	7 0	7 15	...	7 20	3.15 p.m. Camden to Wigan.
Empties ... **C**	...	7 20	...	7 25	For Colwick.
,, ... **C**	...	7 55	...	8 0	,, Doncaster.
Express Pass. ...	8 5	8 7	...	8 11	6.30 p.m. Euston to Rugby.
Pass.	...	8 10	...	8 14	For Harboro'.
,, ...	...	8 10	...	8 14	,, Rugby.
Express Goods **C**	...	...	8 25	8 30	For Rugby.
Ironstone ...	8 20	8 40	...	8 45	8.15 p.m. Bdge. St. to Smethwick.
Express Goods ...	8 35	8 50	...	8 55	8.30 p.m. Bdge. St. to Doncaster.
Empties ... **M**	8 55	9 10	...	9 15	5.45 ,, Willesden to Colwick.
Pass.	9 25	9 30	...	9 34	7.0 ,, Euston to Rugby.
Empties ... **M**	...	9 45	...	9 50	For Colwick.
Express Pass ...	10 31	10 34	...	10 38	9.0 p.m. Euston to Rugby.
Express Goods ...	9 30	11 0	...	11 5	9.25 ,, Bridge St. to Rugby.
,, **M**	...	...	10 47	10 52	7.15 ,, Camden to Birmingham.
,,	11 0	...	...	...	8.0 ,, from Peterboro'.
Empties ...	11 15	11 20	...	11 25	7.35 ,, Willesden to Doncaster.

SUNDAYS.

Description.	Northampton (Castle). arr. a.m.	dep. a.m.	pass a.m.	Kingsthorpe Junction. pass a.m.	Remarks.
Express Goods ...	...	...	12 38	12 38	9.10 p.m. Broad St. to Birminghm.
,, ...	12 35	12 45	...	12 50	9.40 ,, Camden to Doncaster.
Express Pass. ...	1 31	1 33	...	1 37	12.0 night Euston to Rugby.
Express Goods ...	2 8	2 13	...	2 18	11.10 p.m. Camden to Nottinghm.
Goods & Empties...	2 50	3 20	...	3 25	2.45 a.m. Bridge St. to Rugby.
Express Goods **C**	...	3 30	...	3 35	For Doncaster.
Empties	3 40	4 0	...	4 5	12.35 a.m. Willesden to Rugby.
,, ...	4 5	4 10	...	4 15	12.55 ,, ,, Colwick.
,, ...	4 15	4 45	...	4 50	1.0 ,, Camden to Colwick.
,, ...	...	...	5 10.	5 15	For Rugby.
,, ...	8 0	8 10	...	8 15	,, ,,
Pass.	11 25	...	...	...	From Roade.
Express Pass. ..	11 42	11 44	...	11 48	10.0 a.m. Euston to Rugby.
	p.m.				
Pass.	3 47	...	...	...	From Roade.
Express Pass. ...	6 32	6 34	...	6 38	5 0 p.m. Euston to Rugby.
Pass	9 25	9 30	...	9 34	6.45 ,, ,, ,,
Express Pass ...	10 31	10 34	...	10 38	9.0 ,, ,, ,,

D Saturdays excepted.

6

Trains between Kingsthorpe Jun. & Castle Jun., Northampton.

UP TRAINS.

Description.	Kingsthorpe Junction. pass a.m.	Northampton (Castle). arr. a.m.	dep. a.m.	pass a.m.	Remarks.
Express Goods **M**	12 0	...	...	12 5	5.56 p.m. Manchester to Camden.
,, ,, ...	12 47	...	...	12 51	Derby and Leicester to Camden.
Goods ... ... **M**	...	...	1 0	...	12.15 a.m., Blisworth to Bridge Street via Castle, arrive 1.10 a.m., Gas Sidings X.
Express Goods **MM**	2 10	2 15	2 35	...	9.55 p.m. Retford to Camden.
,, ,, **M**	2 24	...	...	2 29	8.50 p.m. Warrington to Camden.
,, ,, **M**	2 35	2 40	4 0	...	10.20 p.m. Wolverhampton to Poplar.
Express Pass. ...	2 56	3 0	3 2	...	1st portion Auxiliary Mail (Does not run on Mondays)
Coal ... ... **M**	3 0	3 5	3 50	...	7.25 p.m. Doncaster to Bletchley.
Fast Goods ... **B**	3 30	3 35	...	...	9.35 p.m. from Doncaster.
Express Pass. ...	3 34	3 38	3 42	...	3.10 a.m. Rugby to Euston.
Coal ... ... **C**	3 15	3 20	...	...	From Colwick.
Exp. Goods ... **M**	3 55	4 0	...	...	11.15 p.m. from Doncaster.
,, ,, **B**	4 0	4 5	4 15	...	3.15 a.m. Rugby to Camden.
,, ,, **M**	...	...	4 30	...	For Peterboro'.
Fast Goods ... **M**	4 25	4 30	5 10	...	3.45 a.m. Rugby to Bridge Street, arrive 5.15 a.m.
Exp. Goods... ...	5 8	...	...	5 13	2.0 a.m. Birmingham to Camden.
Coal	5 25	5 30	5 50	...	1.0 a.m. Colwick to Willesden.
,, ... **M**	5 50	5 55	6 10	...	12.45 a.m. ,, ,,
,, ...	6 10	6 15	6 25	...	2.0 a.m. ,, ,,
,, ... **M C**	6 15	6 20	...	...	From Doncaster.
,, ...	6 40	6 45	7 35	...	5.30 a.m. Rugby to Blisworth.
Coal ... ... **B**	6 35	6 40	7 20	...	2.20 a.m. Colwick to Willesden.
,, ... **M**	6 35	6 40	...	...	From Colwick.
Express Pass. ...	...	...	7 30	...	To London *via* Blisworth.
,, Goods **M**	7 23	...	...	7 28	2.0 a.m. Salop to Camden.
Goods ... ... **M**	6 55	7 0	7 15	...	12.30 a.m. Doncaster to Bridge St., arr. 7.30.
Coal ... ... **C**	7 40	7 45	...	...	From Colwick.
Pass.	7 51	7 55	8 0	...	7.10 a.m. Rugby to Euston.
Goods	...	...	8 10	...	For Peterboro'.
Pass.	8 33	8 36	8 40	...	7.0 a.m. Stamford to Blisworth.
Coal ... **M C**	8 50	8 55	...	...	From Doncaster.
Express Pass. ...	...	...	9 20	...	To London *via* New Line.
Goods ... ... **M**	9 10	9 15	9 25	...	5.15 a.m. B'mingham to Bletchley.
Coal ... ... **C**	9 5	9 10	9 45	...	5.5 a.m. Colwick to Willesden.
Stock Train... ...	9 37	...	...	9 42	1.45 a.m. from Carlisle (commencing July 17th).
Coal ... ... **C**	9 40	9 45	...	...	From Colwick.
,, ... **C**	9 55	10 0	10 10	...	6.0 a.m. Colwick to Bletchley.
Goods and Coal **C**	10 10	...	...	10 15	6.15 a.m. Birmingham to Camden.
Pass.	10 36	10 40	...	...	From Harboro'.
Express Pass. ...	10 44	10 48	10 50	...	9.30 a.m. Birmingham to Euston.
G. N. Pass. ...	11 7	11 11	...	...	From Nottingham.
Pass.	11 9	11 13	...	...	10.33 a.m. from Rugby.
Express Pass. ...	11 15	11 19	11 22	...	7.20 a.m. Liverpool to Euston.
Coal ... ... **C**	12 30	12 35	1 18	...	5.45 a.m. Doncaster to Willesden.
Pass.	12 40	12 43	...	...	From Nottingham.
Express Pass. ...	12 46	12 50	12 53	...	11.30 a.m. Birmingham to Euston.
Express Pass. ...	1 6	1 10	1 13	...	9.45 a.m. Liverpool to Euston.
Goods & Coal ...	1 25	1 30	1 40	...	11.0 a.m. Rugby to Peterboro', arrive Duston North 1.45, depart 1.55.
Coal	1 35	1 40	...	...	From Doncaster.
Express Pass. ...	1 46	1 50	...	...	From Nottingham.
Pass.	1 59	2 3	2 5	...	1.25 Rugby to Euston.
Goods and Coal ...	2 20	2 20	2 25	...	1.30 p.m. Rugby to Maiden Lane.
Coal	2 20	2 25	2 45	...	9.50 a.m. Colwick to Bletchley.
Empties ... **C**	3 13	3 18	3 35	...	Great Bowden to Bridge Street arrive 3.40.
Express Pass. ...	3 43	3 47	3 50	...	3.20 p.m. Rugby to Euston.

B Mondays only.   **D** Saturdays excepted.

7

Trains between Kingsthorpe Jun. & Castle Jun., Northampton.

UP TRAINS—*Continued.*

Description.	Kingsthorpe Junction.	Northampton (Castle).			Remarks.
	pass. p.m.	arr. p.m.	dep. p.m.	pass. p.m.	
Coal ... ... **C**	3 55	4 0	...	...	From Colwick.
Pass.	4 15	4 19	4 20	...	3.35 p.m. Rugby to Blisworth.
Coal ... **D C**	4 40	4 45	4 55	...	12.25 p.m. Colwick to Willesden.
Express Pass. ...	4 48	4 50	4 52	...	11.40 a.m. Holyhead to Euston.
Pass.	5 20	5 24	...	...	From Nottingham.
Express Pass. ...	5 30	5 34	5 36	...	2.5 p.m. Liverpool to Euston.
Coal ... ... **C**	5 40	5 45	6 0	...	10.5 a.m. Doncaster to Willesden.
Pass.	6 6	6 10	...	...	5.25 p.m. *ex* Rugby.
Express Goods **M**	6 15	...	...	6 20	For New Line.
„ **D M**	6 25	...	...	6 30	Second Scotch Goods.
Goods & Empties	6 25	6 30	6 50	...	Great Bowden to Bridge St., arr. 6.55
Coal	7 25	7 30	8 15	...	6.20 p.m. Rugby to Maiden L. *via* Blisworth.
Pass.	7 26	7 30	...	...	From Harboro'.
Coal ... ... **C**	7 50	7 55	...	...	From Doncaster.
Express Pass. ...	8 1	8 5	...	...	From Nottingham.
Coal ... ... **C**	8 15	8 20	8 35	...	4.20 p.m. Colwick to Willesden.
Express Pass. ...	8 26	8 30	8 32	...	5.5 p.m. Liverpool to Euston.
Pass.	9 16	9 20	...	...	From Rugby.
Express Pass. ...	9 32	9 36	9 38	...	6.5 p.m. Liverpool to Euston.
Coal	9 40	9 45	9 55	...	5.30 p.m. Colwick to Willesden.
„ ... ... **D**	10 30	10 35	10 40	...	5.45 p.m. „ „
Express Goods **M**	10 45	...	...	10 50	Irish and Scotch Goods.
Goods	10 5	10 10	11 30	...	9.15 p.m. Rugby to Camden.
Coal & Goods ...	11 40	11 45	12 0	...	10.50 p.m. from Rugby, Gas Sidings arr. 12.5, dep. 12.15, Bridge Street arr. 12.20.

SUNDAYS.

Description.	Kingsthorpe Junction.	Northampton (Castle).			Remarks.
	a.m.	a.m.	a.m,	a.m.	
Express Goods ...	12 0	...	...	12 5	5.56 p.m. Manchester to Camden.
Goods	...	...	1 0	...	12.15 a.m., Blisworth to Bridge Street, *via* Castle, arr. 1.10 a.m., Gas Sidings X.
Express Goods ...	2 28	...	...	2 33	10.20 p.m. W'hampton to Poplar.
„ „ ...	2 38	...	...	2 43	8.50 p.m. Warrington to Camden.
Express Pass. ...	2 56	3 0	3 2	...	2.33 a.m. Rugby to Euston.
Express Goods ...	2 10	2 15	3 5	...	9.55 p.m. Retford to Camden.
Coal	3 0	3 5	3 50	...	7.25 p.m. Doncaster to Bletchley.
Express Pass. ...	3 34	3 38	3 42	...	3.10 a.m. Rugby to Euston.
Express Goods ...	...	...	4 30	...	For Peterboro'.
Fast Goods	4 25	4 30	5 10	...	3.35 Rugby to Bridge St. arr. 5.15 a.m.
Coal	6 35	6 40	6 55	...	2.20 a.m., Colwick to Blisworth.
Fast Goods	7 25	7 30	...	...	From Doncaster.
Goods	8 35	8 40	8 50	...	7.45 a.m. Rugby to Camden.
Pass.	...	...	10 40	...	To Roade.
	p.m.	p.m.	p.m.		
Express Pass. ...	2 59	3 3	3 5	...	11.30 a.m. Liverpool to Euston.
Pass.	...	...	3 10	...	To Roade.
Express Pass. ...	7 49	7 53	7 55	...	4.0 p.m. Liverpool to Euston.

E Wednesdays only.   **G** Saturdays only.

8 BLISWORTH AND NORTHAMPTON.

Distance from Blisworth	STATIONS. WEEK DAYS.—DOWN.		1 Goods.	2	3	4	5	6	7 Goods.	8	9	10	11	12
Miles. 19¼	Rugby ... ...dep.		a.m. ...	...	...	...	...	...	a.m. 3 35	...	...	...	...	...
...	BLISWORTH ... ... „		12 15	...	...	...	...	...	...	...	...	...	...	...
3	Duston Sidings	{ arr.	...	...	...	...	...	...	...	...	...	...	...	...
		{ dep.	M	...	...	...	...	...	M	...	...	...	...	...
4	Duston Junction (West) ...pass		...	...	...	...	...	...	...	...	...	...	...	...
4¼	NORTHAMPTON { (Castle)	{ arr.	12 30	...	...	...	...	...	4 30	...	...	...	...	...
		{ dep.	1 0	...	...	...	...	...	5 10	...	...	...	...	...
	{ (Bridge Street)	{ arr.	1 10	...	...	...	...	...	5 15	...	...	...	...	...
		{ dep.	...	...	...	...	...	...	...	...	...	...	...	...

STATIONS. WEEK DAYS.—DOWN.		13 Goods & Empties.	14 Empties, &c.	15	16	17	18	19	20 Pass.	21	22 Pass.	23	24 Empties.	25 Pass.
Rugby ... ...dep.		a.m. 4 50	a.m. ...	...	...	...	...	...	a.m. ...	...	a.m. ...	...	a.m. ...	a.m. ...
BLISWORTH ... ... „		6 10	...	...	...	...	...	...	9 5	...	9 20	...	...	11 0
Duston Sidings	{ arr.	6 20	...	...	...	...	...	...	...	...	...	...	10 25	...
	{ dep.	6 30	7 20	...	...	...	...	...	...	...	...	...	...	...
Duston Junction (West) ...pass		...	...	...	...	...	...	...	9 12	...	...	...	10 45	11 10
NORTHAMPTON { (Castle)	{ arr.	M	...	...	...	...	...	...	9 14	...	9 30	...	...	
	{ dep.	...	...	...	...	...	...	...	For Har-boro'	...	...	...	For Great Bowden	Wednes. & Sats. excepted
{ (Bridge Street)	{ arr.	6 35	7 25	...	...	...	...	...	...	...	...	...	...	
	{ dep.	...	...	...	...	...	...	...	...	...	...	...	...	

STATIONS. WEEK DAYS.—DOWN.		26 Pass.	27 Pass.	28	29	30	31 Coal.	32 Goods & Empties.	33 Pass.	34	35 Pass.	36 Mineral, &c.	37 Pass.	38
Rugby ... ...dep.		a.m. ...	a.m ...	...	...	...	a.m. 11 0	noon ...	a.m. ...	...	p.m. ...	p.m. ...	p.m. ...	
BLISWORTH ... ... „		11 0	11 35	...	...	...	Via Kings-thorpe.	12 0	1 0	...	1 55	...	3 32	
Duston Sidings	{ arr.	Wednesday and Saturday only.	...	...	...	...		12 10	...	...	...	3 20	...	
	{ dep.		...	...	...	...		12 20	...	...	...	...	...	
Duston Junction (West) ...pass			...	...	...	...		...	1 10	...	2 5	3 40	3 42	
NORTHAMPTON { (Castle)	{ arr.		11 45	...	...	...		...	...	...	...	...	...	
	{ dep.		...	...	...	...		...	...	...	...	...	...	
{ (Bridge Street)	{ arr.	11 10	...	...	...	...	2 0	12 25	...	...	...	...	...	
	{ dep.		...	...	...	...	2 20	...	...	...	...	...	...	

STATIONS. WEEK DAYS.—DOWN.		39 Pass.	40	41 Pass.	42 Pass.	43	44	45 Pass.	46 Pass.	47	48	49	50	51
Rugby ... ...dep.		p.m. ...	...	p.m. ...	p.m. ...	...	...	p.m. ...	p.m. ...	...	...	...	...	...
BLISWORTH ... ... „		4 35	...	6 5	7 15	...	...	7 55	9 5	...	...	...	...	...
Duston Sidings	{ arr.	...	...	...	...	...	...	Sats. only.	...	...	...	...	...	...
	{ dep.	...	...	...	...	...	...		...	...	...	...	...	...
Duston Junction (West) ...pass		...	...	...	...	...	...		...	...	...	...	...	...
NORTHAMPTON { (Castle)	{ arr.	4 45	...	6 15	7 25	...	...	8 5	9 15	...	...	...	...	...
	{ dep.	...	...	...	6.30 p.m ex Bletchley	...	...		...	...	...	...	...	...
{ (Bridge Street)	{ arr.	...	...	...	...	...	...		...	...	...	...	...	...
	{ dep.	...	...	...	...	...	...		...	...	...	...	...	...

STATIONS. SUNDAYS.—DOWN.		1 Goods.	2 Goods.	3	4	5	6	7	8 Empties	9 Engine & Break.	10	11	12	13
Rugby ... ...dep.		a.m. ...	a.m. 3 35	...	...	...	...	...	a.m. 5 5	a.m. ...	...	...	...	...
BLISWORTH ... ... „		12 15	...	...	...	...	...	...	6 20	7 30	...	...	...	...
Duston Sidings	{ arr.	...	...	...	...	...	...	...	6 30		...	...	...	...
	{ dep.	...	...	...	...	...	...	...	6 40		...	...	...	...
Duston Junction (West) ...pass		...	4 30	...	...	...	...	...	3.10 ex Smeth. wick.	Sundays only.	...	...	...	...
NORTHAMPTON { (Castle)	{ arr.	12 30	5 10	...	...	...	...	...			...	...	...	...
	{ dep.	1 0	5 15	...	...	...	...	...	6 45	7 40	...	...	...	...
{ (Bridge Street)	{ arr.	1 10	...	...	...	...	...	...			...	...	...	...
	{ dep.	...	...	...	...	...	...	...			...	...	...	...

* No. 14—2.10 a.m. from Smethwick.

NORTHAMPTON AND BLISWORTH. 9

Distance from N'ampton.	STATIONS. WEEK DAYS—UP.			1 Goods & Empties.	2 Goods.	3	4 Mineral, &c.	5 Coal.	6	7	8 Pass.	9	10 Pass.	11 H'boro Pass.	12
Miles.				a.m.	a.m.	...	a.m.	a.m.	...	...	a.m.	...	a.m.	a.m.	...
	NORTHAMPTON {(Bridge Street)	{arr.		...	M	...	7 0	...	...	...	...	...	8 27	...	...
		{dep.		2 45	4 0	...		...	...	...	...	...	8 30	...	...
	{(Castle)	"			4 30	...		7 35	...	...	7 30	...	...	8 40	...
¾	Duston Junction (West)	...pass		M	...	...		7 38	...	...	...	...	...	7.0 a.m. ex Stamford	...
1¾	Duston Sidings	{arr.		To Rugby.	...	...	7 5	7 40	...	...	...	...	...		...
		{dep.			...	...		7 45	...	...	...	...	...		...
4¾	BLISWORTH ... ...arr.				4 45	...	...	7 55	...	...	7 40	...	8 40	8 50	...
24½	Rugby ... ...arr.			4 15	...	...	...	From Rugby.	...	...	For London	...	...	...	...

STATIONS. WEEK DAYS—UP.			13	14 Empties.	15 Pass.	16	17 Pass.	18 Pass. Wed. and Sat.	19	20	21	22	23	24	25 Pass.
			...	a.m.	a.m.	...	a.m.	a.m.	...	...	...	...	...		p.m.
NORTHAMPTON {(Bridge Street)	{arr.		...	10 0	...	...	...	11 12	...	...	...	...	...	...	...
	{dep.														12 35
{(Castle	"		...	...	10 30	...	11 15	...	...	...	...	...	...	...	
Duston Junction (West)	...pass		...	...	...	...	...	For Castle arr. 11.15.	...	...	...	...	...	...	...
Duston Sidings...	{arr.		...	10 5	...	...	...		...	...	...	...	...	...	...
	{dep.														
BLISWORTH ... ...arr.			For Great Bowden, via Duston.	...	10 40	...	11 25		...	...	...	...	...	...	12 45
Rugby ... ...arr.			...	...	...	...	...		...	...	...	...	...	...	...

STATIONS. WEEK DAYS.—UP.			26 Iron Stone.	27 Pass.	28	29 Empties. &c.	30 Pass.	31	32 Iron Stone, &c.	33 Pass. Weds. and Sats. only.	34	35	36	37 Pass.	38
			p.m.	p.m.	...	p.m.	p.m.	...	p.m.	p.m.	...	...	...	p.m.	...
NORTHAMPTON {(Bridge Street)	{arr.		12 40	...	...	2 0	...	...	3 0	3 10	...	...	...		...
	{dep.		1 0											4 20	
{(Castle)	"		1 10	1 35	...		2 35	...		3 5	...	...	...		...
Duston Junction (West)	...pass		Via Kings-thorpe.	...	...	Via Kings-thorpe.	...	...	3 5	Via Bridge Street.	...	...	3.35 p.m. ex Rugby.		...
Duston Sidings	{arr.			...	...		...	...	3 5		...	...			...
	{dep.														
BLISWORTH ... ...arr.				1 45	...		2 44	...	3 20	3 20	...	...		4 30	...
Rugby ... ...arr.			2 15	...	...	3 50	...	...	...	...	...	...	...	...	...

STATIONS. WEEK DAYS.—UP.			39 Pass.	40	41 Pass.	42	43	44	45 Coal.	46 Pass.	47	48	49 Rugby Goods.	50	51
			p.m.	...	p.m.	...	...	...	p.m.	p.m.	...	...	p.m.	...	...
NORTHAMPTON {(Bridge Street)	{arr.		...	...	...	...	...	...	8 15	8 40	...	...	9 25	...	...
	{dep.		5 45	...	7 40	...	...	...			...	...		...	...
{Castle	"		...	...	...	...	...	...			...	...	Via Kings-thorpe.	...	...
Duston Junction (West)	...pass		...	...	...	...	...	...	7.20 p.m. Rugby to Maiden Lane	Sats. only.	...	...		...	...
Duston Sidings	{arr.		...	...	...	...	...	...			...	...		...	...
	{dep.														
BLISWORTH...	arr		5 55	...	7 50	...	...	...	8 30	8 50	...	...		...	...
Rugby	arr		...	...	...	...	...	...	...	...	...	...	12 0	...	...

STATIONS. SUNDAYS—UP.			1 Goods & Empties.	2 Goods.	3 Coal, Sundays only.	4	5	6	7	8	9	10	11	12	13
			a.m.	a.m.	a.m.	...	...	...	...	...	...	...	...	...	...
NORTHAMPTON {(Bridge Street)	{arr.		2 45	4 0	...	...	...	...	...	...	...	...	...	...	...
	{dep.														
{(Castle	"		...	4 30	6 55	...	...	...	...	...	...	...	...	...	...
Duston Junction (West)	...pass		To Rugby.	...	6 58	...	...	...	...	...	...	...	...	...	...
Duston Sidings...	{arr.			...	7 0	...	...	...	...	...	...	...	...	...	...
	{dep.			...	7 5	...	...	...	...	...	...	...	...	...	...
BLISWORTH ... ...arr.				4 45	7 15	...	...	...	...	...	...	...	...	...	...
Rugby ... ...arr.			4 15	2.20 ex Colwick	...	...	...	...	...	...	...	...	...	...	...

30

DOWN.—WEEK DAYS.
Market Harboro' and Great Bowden Junction.

DESCRIPTION.		Market Harboro'.			Gt. Bowden.
		Pass.	Arr.	Dep.	Pass.
		a.m.	a.m.	a.m.	a.m.
L. & N. W. Empties	A	...	12 10	12 20	12 23
Mid. Express Goods	A	12 13	...	...	12 15
" "	A	12 24	...	...	12 26
Mid. Express Goods	A	12 51	...	...	12 53
L. & N. W. Cattle	C	12 55	...	...	12 58
Mid. Express Goods	A	1 1	...	...	1 3
" "	A	1 19	...	...	1 21
L. & N. W. "	A'	...	1 25	1 35	1 38
Mid. Goods (Mons. only)	A	1 28	...	...	1 31
" Express Goods	A	1 30	...	...	1 33
L. & N. W. Ex. Goods	A	...	1 35	1 45	1 48
Mid. Goods	A	1 40	...	...	1 43
Mid. Express Goods	A	1 48	...	...	1 50
" Express	...	2 4	...	...	2 8
L. & N. W. Empties (Mon. only)	A	...	2 10	2 20	2 23
Mid. Express Goods	A	2 15	...	...	2 17
" " "	A	2 27	...	...	2 30
" " "	A	2 40	...	...	2 42
" " "	A	2 46	...	...	2 48
" Express Goods	A	3 1	...	...	3 3
L. & N.W. Express Goods	A	...	3 5	3 15	3 18
Mid. Goods	A	...	3 15	3 25	3 28
Mid. Express Goods	A	3 21	...	...	3 23
" Goods	A	3 30	...	...	3 33
" Express Goods	A	3 41	...	...	3 44
" "	A	3 48	...	...	3 53
" "	A	4 9	...	...	4 12
" Goods and Mineral	A	4 25	...	...	4 28
L. & N. W. Empties	A C	...	4 35	4 45	4 48
" Goods	A	...	5 5	5 15	5 18
" Empties	A	...	5 15	5 25	5 28
Mid. Goods	A	5 35	...	...	5 33
Mid. Empties	A	5 45	...	...	5 48
L. & N.W. Fast Goods	A	...	5 55	6 5	6 8
" Empties	A	...	5 50	6 15	6 18
" Gds (Mons. only)	...	...	6 0	6 20	6 23
Mid. Express Goods	A C	6 33	...	...	6 35
" "	C	6 56	...	...	6 59
" Goods and Mineral	A	...	6 43	7 0	7 3
L. & N. W. Empties	A	...	6 45	6 55	6 58
Mid. Goods	A	7 15	...	...	7 18
" Passenger	...	...	7 44	7 45	7 47
" Goods	...	7 55	...	...	7 58
L. & N. W. Passenger	...	...	8 15	8 17	8 19
L. & N. W. Goods, &c.	A	...	8 20	8 45	8 48
Mid. Passenger	...	...	8 22	8 24	8 26
L. & N. W. Empties	C A	...	8 30	8 40	8 43
Mid. Express Goods	C A	8 33	...	...	8 36
L. & N. W. Empties	C A	...	8 40	8 50	8 53
Mid. Goods	A	8 50	...	...	8 53
"	C	8 55	...	...	8 58
L. & N. W. Passenger	...	...	9 15	9 16	9 19
" Empties	C	...	9 35	9 45	9 48
Mid. Passenger	...	...	9 44	9 46	9 48
L. & N. W. Passenger	...	...	9 55	...	...
" "	...	...	10 4	10 10	10 12
Mid. Mineral	...	10 12	...	...	10 15
L. & N. W. Empties	C	...	10 15	10 25	10 28
Mid. Goods	A	10 22	...	...	10 25
Mid. Mineral	...	10 28	...	...	10 31
L. & N. W. Empties	C A	...	10 30	10 40	10 43
Mid. Express	...	...	10 44	10 47	10 49
L.&N.W.Emp (Tues. only)	...	...	10 50	11 5	11 8
L. & N. W. Express Pass.	...	...	11 15	11 28	11 30
" Passenger	...	...	11 21	11 23	11 25
" Goods	D	...	11 30	11 45	11 48
Mid. Express	...	11 57	...	...	11 59
		p.m.	a.m.	noon	p.m.
L. & N. W. Empties	C	...	11 35	12 0	12 3
Mid. Scotch Express	...	12 21	...	...	12 22
L. & N. W. Empties	C	...	12 30	12 40	12 43

UP.—WEEK DAYS.
Great Bowden Junction and Market Harboro'.

DESCRIPTION.		Gt. Bowden.	Market Harboro'.		
		Pass.	Pass.	Arr.	Dep.
		a.m.	a.m.	a.m.	a.m.
Mid. Goods	A	12 0	12 3	...	...
" Express Goods	A	12 17	12 19	...	...
" "	A	12 27	12 29	...	...
" Mineral (Mons. only)	...	12 30	12 33	...	...
" Mineral	...	12 37	12 40	...	...
" "	A	12 43	12 45	...	...
" Fish Express	A	12 56	12 58	...	...
L. & N. W. Exp. Goods	A	12 57	...	1 0	1 11
Mid. Express Goods	A R	1 3	1 5	...	...
Mid. Express Goods	A	1 20	1 22	...	...
Mid. Express Goods	A	1 34	1 36	...	...
" Goods	A	1 41	1 43	...	...
L. & N. W. Coal	A	1 47	...	1 50	2 ...
Mid. Express Goods	A	1 53	1 55	...	...
L. & N. W. B'm. Ex. Gds.	A	1 57	...	2 0	2 11
Mid. Express Goods	A	2 0	2 3	...	...
L. & N. W. Coal	C A	2 7	...	2 10	2 20
Mid. Mail	...	2 14	2 15	...	...
L.&N.W. Fast Goods (Mon. only)	D	2 22	...	2 25	2 36
Mid. Mineral	...	2 25	2 28	...	...
Mid. Express Goods	A	2 35	2 37	...	...
L. & N. W. Express Gds.	A	2 57	...	3 0	3 10
Mid. Express	A	3 7	3 8	...	...
" Express Goods (Mon. only)	A	3 9	3 11	...	...
" "	A	3 13	3 15	...	...
Mid. Mineral	...	3 17	3 20	...	...
Mid. Express Goods	...	3 24	3 26	...	...
Mid. Mineral	...	3 42	3 44	...	...
L. & N. W. Coal	...	3 52	...	3 55	4 20
Mid. Mineral	...	4 17	4 20	...	...
L. & N. W. Coal	A	4 32	...	4 35	4 50
Mid. Express Goods	A	4 35	4 37	...	...
L. & N. W. Coal	A	4 52	...	4 55	5 10
Mid. Goods	A	4 55	4 57	...	...
L. & N.W. Coal	A	5 7	...	5 10	5 20
Mid. Mineral	...	5 20	5 23	...	...
L. & N. W. Coal	...	5 22	...	5 25	5 40
Mid. Mineral	A	5 30	5 33	...	...
" "	...	5 41	5 44	...	...
L. & N. W. Goods	A	5 47	...	5 50	6 0
Mid. Scotch Express	...	5 53	5 54	...	...
Mid. Mineral	...	6 17	6 20	...	...
L. & N. W. Goods	S C	6 22	...	6 25	6 35
Mid. Mineral (Mons. only)	...	6 23	6 26	...	...
" Mineral	A	6 25	6 28	...	...
L. & N. W. Coal	C	6 31	...	6 35	6 45
Mid. Express Passenger	...	6 38	...	...	...
Mid. Mineral	...	6 49	...	6 52	7 0
" "	...	7 3	7 6	...	...
L. & N. W. Coal	C A	7 22	...	7 25	7 35
Mid. Mineral	A	7 25	7 28	...	...
L. & N. W. Coal	C	7 42	...	7 45	8 5
Mid. Express	...	7 50	...	7 53	7 55
L. & N. W. Passenger	...	7 54	...	7 56	8 0
" Passenger	...	...	...	...	8 25
" Coal	C	8 27	...	8 30	8 40
" "	C	8 42	...	8 45	8 55
Mid. Express	...	9 25	...	9 27	9 29
L. & N. W. Passenger	...	9 43	...	9 45	9 57
Mid. Express	...	9 49	9 51	...	...
L. & N. W. Passenger	...	9 53	...	9 55	10 5
Mid. Passenger	...	10 15	...	10 17	10 20
" Mineral	...	10 22	10 25	...	...
" "	...	10 31	...	10 34	11 5
G. N. Express Pass.	...	10 43	...	10 45	10 46
L. & N.W. Coal	C	11 7	...	11 25	11 35
Mid. Goods	...	11 10	11 13	...	...
L. & N. W. Passenger	...	11 33	...	11 35	11 37

A—Mondays excepted.   **B**—Saturdays excepted.   **C**—Conditional Trains.   **D**—Mondays only.

31

DOWN.—WEEK DAYS. Market Harboro' and Great Bowden Junction.

DESCRIPTION.		Market Harboro'			Gt. Bowden
		Pass.	Arr.	Dep.	Pass.
		p m	p m	p m	p m
Mid. Mineral		12 45	...	...	12 48
" "		12 55	...	...	12 58
Mid. Passenger		...	1 11	1 13	1 15
L. & N. W. Goods	A	...	1 20	2 0	2 3
G. N. Goods		...	...	1 25	1 28
Mid. Express		...	1 35	1 37	1 39
L. & N. W. Passenger		...	1 40	1 50	1 52
G. N. Passenger		...	1 44	1 45	1 47
Mid. Express		1 52	...	...	1 53
Mid. Mineral		1 55	...	...	1 58
Mid. Goods		...	...	2 5	2 9
L. & N. W. Empties	C	...	2 0	2 10	2 13
Mid. Goods		...	2 10	2 20	2 23
" Express Pass.		...	2 21	2 24	2 26
L.&N.W.Goods&Empties		...	2 25	2 32	2 35
L. & N. W. Empties	C	...	2 35	2 45	2 48
Mid. Goods		...	2 57	3 20	3 23
L. & N. W. Passenger		...	3 17	3 25	3 27
L. & N.W. Empties		...	3 45	3 55	3 58
Mid. Goods		3 50	...	...	3 53
L. & N. W. Empties	C	...	3 55	4 5	4 8
" Express		...	4 27	4 29	4 31
Mid. Mineral		4 35	...	...	4 36
Mid. Express		...	4 56	4 58	5 0
L. & N. W. Ironstone	C	...	5 0	5 10	5 13
Mid. Express		5 22	...	...	5 23
" Goods	A	5 25	...	...	5 28
L. & N. W. Passenger		...	5 34	...	
Mid. "		...	5 41	5 42	5 44
Mid. Empty Carriages		5 46	...	...	5 48
L. & N. W. Empties	C	...	6 10	6 50	6 53
Mid. Passenger		...	6 20	6 24	6 23
L.& N.W.Express Pass.		...	6 30	6 31	6 33
L. & N. W. Passenger		...	6 40	6 41	6 43
"		...	...	6 45	6 47
Mid. Mineral		6 33	...	...	6 36
" "		...	6 36	6 47	6 50
Mid. "		6 53	...	...	6 54
" Mineral		7 0	...	...	7 6
L. & N. W. Empties		...	7 10	7 15	7 18
Mid. Mineral	B	7 20	...	...	7 23
" "		...	7 25	7 35	7 38
L. & N. W. Empties		...	7 30	7 40	7 43
Mid. Mineral		7 50	...	...	7 53
L. & N. W. Passenger		...	7 55	8 10	8 12
Mid. Express Goods		8 6	...	...	8 9
" Express		...	8 17	8 20	8 21
" Goods	B	8 23	...	...	8 26
L. & N. W. Empties	C	...	8 20	8 30	8 33
Mid. Mineral		8 35	...	...	8 38
L. & N. W. Passenger		...	8 55	...	8 38
Mid. Mineral	F	8 58	...	...	
" Empties		9 3	...	...	9 6
L.& N. W. Empties	C	...	8 50	9 10	9 13
Mid. Mineral		9 33	...	...	9 36
L. & N. W. Exp. Goods		...	9 40	9 50	9 53
Mid. Express		9 48	...	...	9 49
" Goods		...	10 5	10 15	10 18
" Mineral		10 20	...	...	10 23
L. & N. W. Empties	A	...	10 10	10 25	10 28
Mid. Mineral	B	10 18	...	...	10 21
" Goods		10 13	...	...	10 26
L. & N. W. Empties	A	...	10 45	10 55	10 58
Mid. Mail		...	10 47	10 49	10 51
L. & N. W. Goods	C	...	10 55	11 0	11 3
Mid. Scotch Express	M	11 12	...	...	11 13
" Goods		11 15	...	...	11 16
Mid. Exp. Goods	A	11 29	...	...	11 31
" "		11 43	...	...	11 45
" "		12 13	...	...	12 15

UP.—WEEK DAYS. Great Bowden Junction and Market Harboro'.

DESCRIPTION.		Gt. Bowden	Market Harboro'		
		Pass.	Pass.	Arr.	Dep.
		a m	a m	a m	a m
Mid. Mineral (attaches at Harboro' on Tuesdays)		11 35	11 38	...	
L. & N. W. Passenger		12 0	...	12 2	12 3
G. N. Goods		12 12	...	12 15	
Mid. Mineral		12 15	12 18	...	
L. & N. W. Coal	C	12 22	...	12 25	12 35
Mid. Goods		12 27	12 30	...	
" Express Pass.		12 40	12 41	...	
"		12 51	...	12 53	12 54
L. & N. W. Coal		12 57	...	1 0	1 20
" Exp. Pass.		1 10	...	1 12	1 20
" "		1 14	...	1 16	1 18
" Empties	C	1 22	...	1 25	1 30
Mid. Mineral		1 57	2 0	...	
" Express		2 14	2 15	...	
" Passenger		2 38	...	2 39	2 41
L. & N. W. Coal		2 39	...	2 42	2 55
Mid. Goods and Mineral		2 47	2 50	...	
L. & N.W. Exp. Pass.		3 5	...	3 7	3 9
Mid. Goods and Mineral		3 12	3 15	...	
L. & N. W. Passenger		3 19	...	3 21	3 25
Mid. Mineral		3 32	3 35	...	
L.&N.W.Goods&Empties		3 42	...	3 45	4 5
" Coal	C B	3 50	...	3 50	4 0
Mid. Express		3 54	3 55	...	
L. & N. W. Coal	C	4 22	...	4 25	4 45
Mid. Mineral		4 17	...	4 20	4 30
L. & N. W. Passenger		4 35	...	4 37	4 40
Mid. Express Goods	A	No	...	4 57	4 58
L. & N. W. Market Train	F	4 55	...	5 2	5 4
Mid. Express		5 0	...	5 10	6 0
L. & N. W. Goods		5 7	...	...	
Mid. Passenger		5 29	...	5 31	5 33
L. & N. W. (Mond. & Frid. only)		5 33	...	5 35	...
Mid. Express Goods	A	5 45	5 47	...	
L. & N. W. Passenger		...	...	...	5 45
Mid. Express		6 24	6 25	...	
L. & N. W. Passenger		...	...	...	6 45
L. & N. W. Coal	C	6 32	...	6 35	6 50
Mid. Scotch Express		6 52	6 53	...	
Mid. Goods		7 2	...	7 5	7 15
L. & N. W. Coal	C	7 5	...	7 8	7 15
Mid. Mineral		7 29	7 32	...	
L. & N. W. Passenger		7 32	...	7 34	7 35
Mid. Express		7 43	7 44	...	
" Mineral		7 47	7 50	...	
L. & N. W. Exp. Pass.		7 26	...	7 28	7 38
" Pass.		8 4	...	8 6	...
Mid. Passenger		8 8	...	8 10	8 14
L. & N. W. Exp. Goods	B	8 27	...	8 30	8 35
L. & N. W. Coal		8 32	...	8 35	8 45
Mid. Mineral		8 42	8 45	...	
L. & N. W. Goods		8 47	...	8 50	9 15
Mid. Mineral		8 50	8 53	...	
L. & N. W.	B	9 24	...	9 27	9 35
Mid. Mineral		9 35	9 38	...	
" Express Goods	B	9 35	...	...	
" Mineral		10 7	10 10	...	
" Goods		10 16	10 19	...	
" Express Goods	B	10 50	11 0	...	
" Mineral	B	11 6	11 9	...	
L. & N. W. Fish	C	11 15	...	11 17	11 22
Mid. Passenger		11 20	...	11 22	11 25
" Express Goods	B	11 25	11 28	...	
" Mineral		11 37	11 40	...	
" Express Goods	B	11 49	11 52	...	
L. & N. W. Fast Goods		11 52	...	11 55	12 20

F—Frids. and Sats. excepted.　G—Suns. and Mons. excepted.　I—Weds. only.
M—Stops to take up Passengers for Carlisle and beyond.　N—Tues. excepted.　X—Stops to take up London Passengers.　P—Tues. only.　R.—Detaches Cattle if required.　S—Runs regularly on Mondays.

32

DOWN.—SUNDAYS. Market Harboro' and Great Bowden Junction.					UP.—SUNDAYS. Great Bowden Junction and Market Harboro'.				
DESCRIPTION.		Market Harboro'.		Gt. Bow-den.	DESCRIPTION.		Gt. Bow-den.		Market Harboro'.	
	Pass.	Arr.	Dep.	Pass.		Pass.	Pass.	Pass.	Arr.	Dep.
	a m	a m	a m	a m		a m	a m	a m	a m	a m
L. & N. W. Empties ...	...	12 10	12 20	12 22	Mid. Mineral	...	12 42	12 45	...	...
Mid. Express Goods......	...	12 34	...	12 36	„ Fish Express	...	12 56	12 58	...	...
„ „	...	12 51	...	12 53	L. & N. W. Express Goods	...	12 57	...	1 0	1 10
L. & N. W. Cattle C	12 55	...	...	12 58	Mid.	...	1 2	1 5	...	...
Mid. Express Goods......	...	1 1	...	1 3	„ „	...	1 18	1 21	...	...
„ „	...	1 19	...	1 21	Mid. Express Goods......	...	1 47	1 50	...	...
„ „	...	1 30	...	1 32	L. & N. W. Coal	...	1 47	...	1 50	2 5
L. & N. W. „ „	...	1 35	1 45	1 48	„ Exp. Goods	...	1 57	...	2 0	2 15
Mid. „ „	...	1 48	...	1 50	Mid. Mail	...	2 14	2 15	...	...
Mid. Express.........	...	2 4	...	2 5	„ Mineral	...	2 24	2 27	...	...
„ „ Goods......	...	2 15	...	2 17	„ Goods	...	2 50	2 53	...	...
„ „ „	...	2 27	...	2 29	„ Express..........	...	3 7	3 8	...	...
„ „ „	...	2 40	...	2 42	„ „ Goods......	...	3 9	3 11	...	...
„ „ „	...	2 46	...	2 48	„ Mineral	...	3 43	3 45	...	...
„ „ „	...	3 1	...	3 3	Mid. Mineral..........	...	4 36	4 39	...	...
L. & N. W. Express Goods	...	3 5	3 15	3 18	Mid. Goods and Mineral	...	5 7	5 10	...	...
Mid. „ „	...	3 15	3 25	3 28	„ „	...	5 25	5 28	...	...
„ „ „	...	3 21	...	3 23	L. & N. W. Goods & Coal	...	5 22	...	5 25	5 45
„ Goods	...	3 30	...	3 33	Mid. Scotch Express ...	...	5 53	5 54	...	...
„ Express Goods	...	3 38	...	3 40	L. & N. W. Fast Goods	...	6 12	...	6 15	6 25
„ „ „	...	3 48	...	3 50	Mid. Express Passenger	...	6 37	6 38	...	...
„ Goods and Mineral	...	4 9	...	4 12	„ Mineral	...	7 25	7 28	...	...
L. & N. W. Empties...... C	...	4 25	4 35	4 38	„ Passenger........	...	8 49	...	8 51	8 53
„ „	...	5 15	5 25	5 28	„ Express..........	...	9 26	9 27	...	...
Mid. Empties.........	...	5 35	...	5 38			p.m.	p.m.	p.m.	p.m.
L. & N. W. Empties......	...	...	5 40	5 50	5 53	„ „	...	3 5	3 6	...	...
Mid. Goods and Mineral	...	...	5 55	6 5	6 8	„ „ Goods......	...	4 49	4 51	...	...
L. & N. W. Fast Goods ...	...	...	5 55	6 8	6 11	L. & N. W. Passenger ..	...	6 6	...	...	6 0
L. & N. W. B'ham Goods	...	...	6 50	7 0	7 3	Mid. Passenger........	...	6 6	...	6 8	6 10
Mid. Goods and Mineral	...	6 53	...	...	6 56	„ Express Goods......	...	6 17	6 19	...	...
„ Goods and Mineral	...	7 28	...	...	7 31	„ „	...	7 50	...	7 52	7 53
„ Goods	...	8 8	...	...	8 11	Mid. Express Goods......	...	8 26	8 28	...	...
„ „	...	9 47	...	...	9 50	„ Express Goods......	...	10 13	10 15	...	...
„ Passenger..........	...	...	11 9	11 12	11 14	„ Express Goods......	...	10 44	10 46	...	...
		p.m.	p m	p m	p.m.	„ Goods and Mineral	...	11 10	11 12	...	...
„ Express	...	...	4 44	4 46	4 48	„ „ „	...	11 26	11 29	...	...
„ „	...	5 2	...	...	5 3	„ „ „	...	11 41	11 44	...	...
L. & N. W. Cattle & Goods	...	...	6 40	6 50	6 53	L. & N. W. Exp. Goods	...	11 52	...	11 55	12 5
Mid. Express Goods......	...	7 30	...	...	7 22						
L. & N. W. Passenger ...	...	...	8 20	...	...						
Mid. Passenger..........	...	...	9 4	9 6	9 8						
„ Mineral	...	9 27	...	...	9 30						
„ „	...	10 32	...	...	10 35						
„ Mail	...	...	10 47	10 49	10 51						
Mid. Scotch Express ...	...	11 11	...	...	11 12						

LIST OF BALLAST AND PERMANENT WAY STORES TRAINS.

No.	Description.	Between what points running.
1, 2, & 3	Ballast	Blisworth, Peterboro', Rugby, Melton Mowbray, and Luffenham, *via* Northampton, Market Harboro', Yarwell Junction, &c.
4	Do.	Leighton and Elton Ballast Pit.
5	Do.	Leamington and Welford.
1	Material	Northampton, Rockingham, Harboro', &c.

33

NOTICE TO STATION AGENTS, BREAKSMEN, AND OTHERS.

Goods, &c., Trains to be marshalled as under :—

2.10 a.m., Smethwick to Northampton (via Blisworth).—Works Waggons for exchange at Coventry, Rugby, and Blisworth, and for Local Stations on Peterboro' Branch to go forward from Northampton by 9.30 a.m. Train. Iron Stone Empties for Bevans, Blisworth, N. & B. Line, and Duston Sidings to be worked by this Train.

8.50 p.m., Birmingham to Peterboro'.—Traffic for Peterboro' and beyond, and exchange at Harboro' Great Eastern Empties. Lime Traffic, Barnston to Norwich, to be worked by this Train from Market Harboro'.

1.0 a.m., Camden to Colwick.—To Convey traffic for Peterboro' Line and Northampton to Castle Station, and from there Empties brought by 12.55 a.m. from Willesden.

9.40 p.m., Camden to Doncaster.—With traffic for Lancashire and Yorkshire and North Eastern Lines, and for exchange with Manchester Sheffield and Lincolnshire Company at Retford. Traffic for Lincoln to be worked to Retford. Train to be marshalled as follows :—Retford, Lincoln, Sheffield, Lancashire and Yorkshire, North Eastern, Waggons for Doncaster proper, break.

11.10 p.m., Camden to Nottingham.—Waggons from Northampton for Stamford Branch, King's Cliffe, Market Harboro', and Nottingham District, and Parcels Van for Nottingham, to be attached to this Train at Castle Station. Works sheeted goods, &c., for Nottingham brought to Market Harboro' by 8.50 p.m. Train from Birmingham. Late Goods Traffic for Sheffield, Lancashire and Yorkshire and North Eastern Lines, and Newark Waggons from Camden, to be worked by this Train to Stathern, thence by 7.35 p.m. ex Willesden.

1.0 a.m., Colwick to Camden.—To work fish traffic for Northampton, brought to Harboro' by 12.30 a.m. from Peterboro'.

2.20 a.m., Colwick to Northampton.—Coal Traffic for Heyford. Great Northern Goods Traffic for Melton and Northampton. When short of load to take Coal for Stamford, Seaton and Wansford, Rugby and Northampton Lines. On Sundays to work Fish Traffic for Northampton brought to Harboro' by 12.30 a.m. from Peterboro', and run to Blisworth with Heyford, &c., Traffic.

5.30 p.m., Colwick to Willesden.—Coal for C Sidings and North London Line ; and when not a full load of this description of traffic, Camden Coal to be attached. A full load of Coal for B Sidings to be worked on the Train if not sufficient of the first mentioned traffic for a full Train.

11.15 p.m., Doncaster to Northampton (12.15 a.m. Sundays).—Traffic for exchange at Market Harboro', Northampton, &c., Bletchley, and via Bletchley, local Stations South of Bletchley, Willesden, and via Willesden, Camden, and other London Stations, to go forward from Northampton by 10.20 p.m. from Wolverhampton, except that on 12.15 a.m. on Sundays, which must be attached to 7.45 a.m. ex Rugby. On Sundays to work G. N. Traffic from Newark to Northampton.

12.30 a.m., Doncaster to Northampton.—Great Northern Goods Traffic from Newark, &c., to Northampton, making up with London Coal traffic.

6.15 a.m., Doncaster to Northampton.—To work Coal Traffic for Stamford, Seaton and Wansford, Rugby and Northampton Lines, Duston Sidings, and Ironstone Traffic for Duston Sidings and Heyford.

4.30 a.m., Northampton to Peterboro'.—With traffic for Branch Stations where timed, Peterboro' and Great Eastern Line.

10.15 a.m., Northampton to Great Bowden.—With Traffic for Market Harboro', to and from all stations where timed to stop and to work traffic between Brixworth and Harboro' for Stations on the Rugby side of Harboro'.

2.0 p.m., Northampton to Rugby.—Work Pig Iron, &c., Traffic from Peterboro' Branch brought by 6.0 a.m. Train ex Peterboro', and make up load at Castle Station with same class of Traffic. Train to be marshalled as follows on leaving Castle Station :— Engine Waggons for transfer at Coventry, South Stafford, also G.W. via Dudley and Bushbury, Stour Valley Waggons, Bloomfield to Wolverhampton inclusive ; Stour Valley Waggons, Monument Lane to Tipton inclusive, those for South Wales via Smethwick Junction together, Waggons for Birmingham proper and Midland System on Break Van.

2.40 p.m., Northampton to Retford.—Empties for South Yorkshire Collieries via Retford, brought by 9.30 a.m. ex Willesden. Cattle Traffic from Northampton on Wednesdays and Saturdays for Joint Line, and Stations between Rugby and Stamford.

8.30 p.m., Northampton to Doncaster.—Great Northern Traffic from Northampton to be worked by this Train ; N. E. & M. S. & L. Empties brought to Northampton by 6.0 a.m. ex Peterboro' to be made up with Coal Empties for Doncaster District.

9.25 p.m., Northampton to Rugby.—With traffic for Rugby and beyond (Sheeted Waggons and important Goods only). To be marshalled as follows at Bridge Street :—Engine, Leeds, Harboro' Line, Rugby, Manchester, Leicester, and Liverpool.

34

9.20 p.m., Nottingham to Rugby.—London and South Traffic to be transferred at Melton Mowbray to 9.55 p.m. from Retford. Works Parcels Van, Nottingham to Rugby.

12.30 a.m., Peterboro' to Birmingham.—Traffic for Walsall, Great Bridge, and South Stafford District from Peterboro' District to be detached at Rugby, and sent forward by 12.15 a.m., Camden to Walsall Train. Fish Traffic for Northampton, &c., to be worked to Market Harbro' by this Train.

6.0 a.m., Peterboro' to Rugby, Via Northampton.—To convey Pig Iron, &c., Traffic for Birmingham District from Peterboro' Branch, to go forward from Bridge Street by 2.0 p.m. Train, and do the local work at all Stations where timed. Detach all Empty Waggons at Thrapston, except those for Mid. Line; work Ironstone from Newbridge Siding for Mid. Line; Ironstone from Ringstead, and Limestone from Higham for Butlin's Siding; Limestone, Higham for Duston Siding. Clear Butlin's Siding daily of all Pig Iron, &c., Traffic for Birmingham District.

1.0 p.m., Peterboro' to Rugby, Via Seaton.—With Traffic to and from Stations where timed. To leave Peterboro' with not more than 10 through Waggons, so as to do the work properly at the Stations on the way.

5.20 p.m., Peterboro' to Northampton (C.).—Goods, &c., Traffic for North, Birmingham District, &c., from Stations where timed, from and to Local Stations, Empty Goods Waggons, and Empty Coal Waggons from Thrapston. Train to be marshalled, Engine, Traffic for exchange at Bridge Street, Broad Street Tariff Van, Banbury Tariff Van, Nottingham Tariff Van, Roadside Waggons for New Line, Traffic for exchange at Rugby, Manchester, Liverpool, Birmingham and District.

8.0 p.m., Peterboro' to Northampton (C.).—With traffic for London, for Trent Valley Line from Wansford and Stations forward, Waggons for Broad Street to be marshalled together, and the same with each other London Station. Train to be marshalled, Engine, Broad Street, Camden, Willesden via Bletchley, and for exchange at Northampton.

7.20 p.m., Peterboro to Rugby, Via Seaton.—To be made up with through load on leaving Peterboro' and Wansford for Rugby and beyond as far as possible, working Traffic to Market Harbro', only in connection with 9.40 p.m. Camden to Doncaster, and 11.10 p.m. Camden to Nottingham. (*See Special Instructions, for Loading during Fruit Season.*)

9.55 p.m., Retford to Camden.—With traffic from Retford, Newark, for *via* Bletchley and Local Stations South, to be detached at Bletchley, and for all London Stations in marshalled order; also conveys Traffic for London and Stations south of Bletchley transferred from 9.20 p.m. from Nottingham at Melton.

3.35 a.m., Rugby to Northampton.—Leeds, Manchester, Liverpool, and Leicester Waggons to be marshalled together at Rugby and placed in Shed Roads at Castle Station by Train Engine.

6.15 a.m., Rugby to Stamford.—(4.45 a.m. on Mondays) works Traffic for Stations between Harbro' and Melton for exchange at Harbro' and Stations where timed.

4.0 a.m. Rugby to Peterboro.—(6.0 a.m. on Sundays.) To work Traffic for Harbro' proper, Traffic for Stamford detached at Market Harbro' from 11.10 p.m. ex Camden, and for Peterboro' and beyond.

11.0 a.m., Rugby to Peterboro'.—Iron Stone Empties for Cogenhoe, Wellingboro', Butlin's Siding, Whitehouses, and Rixon's Sidings, Newbridge, &c. Coal for Stations on New Line, Duston Sidings, Gas Works, Bridge Street, and Peterboro' Branch to Wansford.

11.20 a.m., Rugby to Peterboro'.—Traffic to and from Stations where timed. On Mondays leaves at 9.30 a.m. to work Cattle Traffic for Harbro', Peterboro', Notts Joint Line, and Eastern Counties.

6.45 p.m., Stamford to Rugby.—With traffic to and from Stations where timed to call. London traffic to be left at Harbro' for the 9.55 p.m. from Retford.

4.20 a.m., Stathern to Nottingham (Mondays only).—Late Nottingham traffic attached at Northampton, Harboro', and Melton, to 1.15. a.m. *ex* Northampton.

3.30 p.m., Thrapston to Northampton.—Coal Empties for Doncaster and Colwick Districts to go on by proper Trains from Northampton, and make up load with Ironstone, &c., for Birmingham District, to go on by 8.15 p.m. from Bridge Street.

7.35 p.m., Willesden to Doncaster.—North Eastern Empty Waggons from Southern Division. Newark Traffic, and late Goods Traffic for Sheffield, Lincoln, Doncaster, &c., worked to Stathern by 11.10 p.m. *ex* Camden.

Index of Persons

(Douglas Thompson)